The FAITH and VALUES of SARAH PALIN

The FAITH and VALUES of SARAH PALIN

STEPHEN MANSFIELD
and DAVID A. HOLLAND

A STRANG COMPANY

Most STRANG COMMUNICATIONS BOOK GROUP products are available at special quantity discounts for bulk purchase for sales promotions, premiums, fundraising, and educational needs. For details, write Strang Communications Book Group, 600 Rinehart Road, Lake Mary, Florida 32746, or telephone (407) 333-0600.

THE FAITH AND VALUES OF SARAH PALIN
    by Stephen Mansfield and David Holland
Published by FrontLine
A Strang Company
600 Rinehart Road
Lake Mary, Florida 32746
www.strangbookgroup.com

Unless otherwise noted, all Scripture quotations are from the Holy Bible, New International Version. Copyright © 1973, 1978, 1984, International Bible Society. Used by permission.

Scripture quotations marked NAS are from the New American Standard Bible. Copyright © 1960, 1962, 1963, 1968, 1971, 1972, 1973, 1975, 1977 by the Lockman Foundation. Used by permission. (www.Lockman.org)

Cover design by Bill Johnson

Library of Congress Cataloging-in-Publication Data

Mansfield, Stephen, 1958-
    The faith and values of Sarah Palin / Stephen Mansfield and David A. Holland. -- 1st ed.
        p. cm.
    Includes bibliographical references and index.
    ISBN 978-1-61638-164-6
    1. Palin, Sarah, 1964---Religion. 2. Palin, Sarah, 1964---Ethics. 3. Palin, Sarah, 1964---Political and social views. 4. Social values--United States--Case studies. 5. Republican Party (U.S. : 1854-)--History. 6. Women governors--Alaska--Biography. 7. Vice-Presidential candidates--United States--Biography. I. Holland, David A. II. Title.
    F910.7.P35M36 2010
    979.8'052092--dc22
    [B]
                                                    2010024744

First Edition

10 11 12 13 14 — 9 8 7 6 5 4 3 2 1
Printed in the United States of America

Contents

To Bev and Tracy

Introduction

Our political anger is only the most impressive expression of a much wider cultural transformation. In politics, in music, in sports, on the web, in our families, and in the relations between the sexes, American anger has come into its own.[1]

—STANLEY KURTZ

WE LIVE IN AN *AMERICAN IDOL* NATION. WE OBSERVE. WE pass judgment. We vote on. We vote off. And when the decision is made, with next week's stars duly chosen, we believe that truth has prevailed.

Yet truth is not found in the liking or the disliking. It is not found in the act of choosing whom we prefer. Instead, truth is found in what the broader experience means for our lives and our culture. What is it about our society, for example, that has allowed *American Idol* and its contrived competition between singers to become a record-breaking national addiction? If truth is to be found here at all, surely it is lurking in this question of meaning rather than in the shallow matter of our personal preferences for aspiring stars.

The same may be said of Sarah Palin's emergence upon our national stage. From the moment she joined John McCain on the Republican ticket in 2008, Palin stirred a firestorm of emotion rarely seen in American politics. Former Texas congressman Dick Armey has quipped, "If I am sitting with ten Republicans in a room and the subject of Sarah Palin comes up, you can bet there is going to be an argument. Some will hate her. Some will see her nearly as a savior. But you can bet there is going to be a fight."[2] This has become our national experience. Palin is unquestionably among the most incendiary figures in our public life, and, just as with *American Idol*, the national focus has largely been upon her polarizing effect, upon the liking or the disliking of who she is and what she represents.

These passions she arouses have fed into the rage and anger that have become our culture's most common forms of expression, particularly in the arena of politics. Even some of our most reasoned commentators have veered into imbalance. Let Sarah Palin scribble some notes on her hand before a Tea Party speech in Nashville, and Chris Matthews—host of one of MSNBC's flagship programs—strays into the bizarre: "Can a palm reader be president? What do we think of kids in school who write stuff on their hands to get through a test? What do we think of a would-be political leader who does it to look like she's speaking without notes?"[3]

A "palm reader"?

Then consider this from eminent commentator Andrew Sullivan. Keep in mind that Sullivan was educated at Oxford. He studied at Harvard. He writes for one of the nation's premier magazines, *The Atlantic*. Yet, in an article on Palin, Sullivan seems to have forgotten himself.

> Here's a revealing glimpse into how a delusional, incompetent, pathological liar has managed never to hold a real press conference and yet remains a credible public figure. She avoids the filters.... The problem here is not really Palin. Every delusional, ignorant nutcase should have a chance to get away with running for national office.[4]

These, though, are the passions of the overheated popularity contest, of American politics conducted at the most superficial level of *American Idol*. It is evidence of journalists abandoning the better angels of their nature and fulfilling the prophetic utterance of author Peter Wood in his *A Bee in the Mouth: Anger in America Now*: "For the first time in our political history, declaring absolute hatred for one's opponent has become a sign not of sad excess but of good character."[5]

Yet, as with *American Idol*, there is a deeper meaning. The truth is that when Sarah Palin stepped onto our national stage, she also stepped onto cultural fault lines that reveal much about who we are and where we are heading as a country. This is where the more critical meaning of Sarah Palin in our national life resides, and it is a meaning that goes beyond like and dislike to the very definition of what it means to be an American.

Consider for a moment the urban/rural divide in our nation. Though 80 percent of the U.S. population is living in urban centers, most have moved from rural areas during their lifetimes and are but one generation removed from farm life.[6] Sarah Palin ought not have been that foreign, then, to the average American. She had grown up in rural Alaska and had a decidedly small-town, even rustic early life. Her accent, shaped as it was by Scandinavian, Russian, and Eskimo dialects, was unfamiliar to many in the Lower 48 states but was not so odd as to repel.

Yet Palin's rural roots have been so harshly treated by an urban media elite that it ought to make Americans who identify with small-town life wonder what has happened to their country. Pulitzer Prize–winning columnist Maureen Dowd called Palin a "Caribou Barbie."[7] Mitch Marconi of the *Post Chronicle* referred to the former Alaska governor as "trailer trash."[8] A *Newsweek* cover story proclaimed "She's One of the Folks (And That's the Problem)," and editor Jon Meacham derisively wrote in the accompanying article, "Palin sometimes seems an odd combination of Chauncey Gardiner from 'Being There' and Marge from 'Fargo.'"[9] And in the esteemed *New York Times*, media writer David Carr suggested that Palin prompted "a lot of sniggering in media rooms and satellite trucks about her beauty queen looks and rustic hobbies, and the suggestion that she was better suited to be a calendar model for a local auto body shop than a holder of the second-highest office in the land."[10]

This in a country that thinks of itself in terms of rural values, that vaunts "small-town America," and whose very Declaration of Independence was penned by a man who said, "Those who labour in the earth are the chosen people of God."[11] Yet these are typical of the passions that Sarah Palin incites, passions that reveal a nation angrily in tension with itself.

Consider too the matter of religion. The Pew Forum on Religion and Public Life has for years reported that most Americans believe in God, identify with a traditional religion, and prefer that their elected leaders do likewise. Again, Palin ought to have been a natural fit. She was raised in a mainline denomination and, though an evangelical, had proven herself balanced and even deferential on matters of homosexuality and creationism while serving as Alaska's governor.

Yet she has been attacked for her faith and her Pentecostal roots as though she is an inflamed member of the Taliban. Indeed, Juan Cole of the Middle East Studies department at Michigan University has written an article for the online *Salon* magazine entitled "What's the Difference Between Palin and Muslim Fundamentalists? Lipstick." The subtitle insists, "A theocrat is a theocrat, whether Muslim or Christian."[12] The influential news and commentary Web site *The Daily Beast* described Palin as an "evangelical foot soldier who spearheaded the [conservative Christian] movement's takeover of local government," as the duped follower of an African witch hunter, and as a heretic who believes that Satan had sex with Eve in the Garden of Eden and thus gave birth to "all the smart, educated people."[13] Influential blogger James Howard Kunstler has called Palin and her followers "corn-pone Nazis" who are given to "Jesus tub-thumping" and "religious paranoia."[14]

This in a nation whose founding Declaration argues that there is a God who rules both nature and the destinies of men, in a land settled initially by refugees seeking an escape from religious intolerance. Clearly, these pillars of our founding are no longer defining factors in America today, and Sarah Palin has exposed this religious fault line in our culture just as she has so many others.

Then there is the matter of Palin's politics. Today she is the symbolic leader of a Tea Party movement that is threatening to evolve into a third party on the right wing of the American political spectrum. Having campaigned at the side of moderate John McCain and for a Republican Party in disarray, she has found both wanting and has chosen to lend her fire to a reform effort devoted to limited government, low taxes, and free markets. This is her natural ideological home, and these are the values upon which, in large part, she built her successful political career in Alaska.

Yet critics have raged, accusing both Palin and the movement of being racist, reactionary, and repugnant to the Constitution. James Kunstler has screeched that the Tea Party's vision of America is "a weird contradictory mish-mash of Confederate nostalgia, hyperindividualism that really owes allegiance to nothing, racial enmity, religious paranoia, and Potemkin patriotism—especially involving anything in the Constitution that allows them to wriggle out of obligations to the public interest at the same time that they get to push other groups of people around."[15] Even Speaker of the House Nancy Pelosi has called the Tea Party an "Astroturf" movement rather than a grassroots movement, meaning that it was created by the wealthy to avoid taxes rather than by the common man to reform government.[16]

Even here, Palin has put her foot upon a surprising fault line. The Tea Party is not a movement of the wealthy, or even of the Southern and the religious, whom Kunstler derides. Instead, the movement boasts a significant number of Democrats, has won a substantial following in traditionally left-leaning northern states like Oregon and Massachusetts, and, surprisingly, is a movement of women more than men. As of mid-2010, most of its board members were women, most of its state coordinators were women, most of its audience were women, and its two brightest stars were Congresswoman Michele Bachmann of Minnesota and Sarah Palin of Alaska.[17] Moreover, rather than reflecting the values of the once powerful religious Right, the movement has been strategically silent on matters of abortion and homosexuality in hopes of preserving unity around its central theme of fiscal responsibility. Clearly, there is a realignment occurring in American politics, and once again Sarah Palin has helped to expose it.

There is likely much more exposure of America's cultural tectonic plates to come. Palin is an attractive, successful woman who rejects the values of feminism and yet may try to shatter the last glass ceiling in America—the one that protects the American presidency. She is a cultural conservative who is a mother of five and who, by all accounts, has been faithful to her high-school-sweetheart husband. Yet she has had to contend with a late-night-talk-show host calling her a "slut" and with vile depictions of herself in porn films. She is also an intelligent, well-read woman who has, admittedly, flubbed some critical interviews, making her look ignorant and incurious. She surely longs for a day of redemption, if not retribution. More importantly, she is antiabortion and pro-gun in a nation where both are legal but in question, and she is a private property advocate while from an Alaska in which all but 1 percent of the land is owned by state, federal, and tribal governments.[18]

Even her seeming contradictions hold wider import. She is a big business advocate and a union member. She is a patriotic American and yet is married to a man who once advocated independence for Alaska. She is a Republican and yet helped send corrupt Republicans to prison.

Clearly, there are more fault lines that Sarah Palin is likely to expose, more political rage coming her way. Yet this may well assure that some of the most important questions of our political life are aired. Is American culture such that a candidate for high office, if a conservative Christian, has to run away from her faith in order to win? Indeed, can a Pentecostal aspire to high office in this country? Do we elect officials for their political values and moral compass, or do we elect them for their mastery of the knowledge they will need while in office? Will the politics of personal destruction, what some call *the criminalization of politics*, drive the best of us from public life? Will we only have the polished, the wealthy, and the finely schooled lead us; or can the intelligent, principled, but rougher sort play a role? Can an attractive woman run for public office without being sexually abused in popular entertainment and media?

These are but a few of the matters of consequence that Palin's presence in our national life raises, and these too are the matters that have prompted this book. As a result, what follows here is neither biography nor commentary alone, but rather a reappraisal. Political preferences aside, is it possible to consider the truth of Sarah Palin's story—its nobility, its disappointments, its drama, and its lessons—as a reflection upon American culture and the direction of American society? This is the attempt here, before the next chapter of her life unfolds yet while memories of the 2008 election are fresh and while its repercussions daily define the America our generation will bequeath to generations yet unborn. In short, what do Sarah Palin's faith and values tell us about America?

Section 1

BEGINNINGS

Chapter 1

ROOTS OF FAITH AND DARING

Do not handicap your children by making their lives easy.[1]
—ROBERT A. HEINLEIN

It is a warm summer day in June of 1964, and at Christ the King Roman Catholic Church in Richland, Washington, a tender moment is unfolding. A small group of the faithful has gathered before a candled altar and a patiently waiting priest. Though the church is spare, it is transformed into regal splendor by the color of deep green evidenced in the vestments of the priest and in the cloth that adorns the altar. This is the color that the Christian church has used for centuries to signify the liturgical season of Pentecost, in which the coming of God's Spirit is celebrated, in which refreshing and new birth are the themes. It is a fitting symbolism for today's event, for a child is soon to be baptized.

When all are settled, the priest steps to the fore and nods his head to a young family. They move, solemnly, to the baptismal font—a father, a mother, a two-year-old boy, a one-year-old girl, and the infant who is the object of today's attention.

"Peace be with you," the good priest begins.

"And also with you," those gathered respond.

"And what is the child's name?" the priest asks.

"Sarah Louise Heath," comes the answer.

"And what is your name?" the priest asks the parents.

The answer comes, but it is obvious to all that the energetic part of that answer, the one filled with eagerness and faith, has come from the child's mother. She is a striking figure. Slightly taller than her husband, she is lean and feminine, possessing a sinewy strength that is unusual for a mother of three. Her eyes are intelligent, slightly wearied but quick to flash into joy. Her mouth is wise, reflecting a sense of the irony in the world and yet disarmingly sweet.

It is her voice, though, that her children and her friends will comment upon most throughout her life. It has a musical lilt that rises and falls with meaning and emotion. It makes the most mundane statement a song, transforming a book read to children before bed or a prayer said before a family meal into a work of art.

This young mother was born Sally Ann Sheeran in 1940 and so took her place in a large, proud, well-educated Irish Catholic family in Utah. As would become the pattern of her life, she would not be there long. When she was three, her family moved to Richland, Washington. Her father, known to friends as Clem, had taken a job as a labor relations manager at the Washington branch of the Manhattan Project, whose task it was to perfect the atomic bomb sure to be needed before the Second World War, then well underway, was over. From her father, Sally acquired a passion for doing things well, a love of sports, and unswerving devotion to Notre Dame, a loyalty questioned in the Sheeran home only at great peril.

It was Sally's mother, Helen, who taught her the domestic skills and devotion to community that would become her mainstays in the years ahead. Helen was widely known as a genius with a sewing machine and made clothes not only for her own family but also for dozens of others in her town. She also had an uncanny ability to upholster furniture. Neighbors remember the astonishing quality of her work and how she refused payment, though her fingers were often swollen and bleeding from the hours she spent stretching leather over wooden frames or forcing brass tacks into hardened surfaces. Helen taught her children the joy of the simple task done well, that the workbench and the desk are also altars of God not too unlike the altar at the Catholic church they attended every week.

Sally came of age, then, in a raucous, busy family of overachievers. There were piano lessons and sports and pep squads and sock hops. Achievement was emphasized. All the Sheeran children did well. Sally's brother even earned a doctorate degree and became a judge. Sally herself finished high school and then began training as a dental assistant at Columbia Basin College.

"What are you asking of God's church?" the priest intones from the ancient Latin text.

"Faith," respond the child's parents.

"What does faith hold out to you?" he asks.

"Everlasting life," they answer.

"If, then, you wish to inherit everlasting life, keep the commandments, 'Love the Lord your God with all your heart, with all your soul, and with all your mind; and your neighbor as yourself.'"

At this moment the priest leans over young Sarah, still in her mother's arms, and breathes upon her three times. "Depart from her, unclean spirit, and give place to the Holy Spirit, the Advocate."

It is then that he traces the sign of the cross upon the child's forehead and prays, "Lord, if it please you, hear our prayer, and by your inexhaustible power protect your chosen one, Sarah, now marked with the sign of our Savior's holy cross. Let her treasure this first sharing of your sovereign glory, and by keeping your commandments deserve to attain the glory of heaven to which those born anew are destined; through Christ our Lord."

At these words, some who have gathered shift their eyes to the young father of the child being baptized. His name is Chuck. He is a good man, all agree, and he loves his family, but he is only tolerant of his wife's faith. He does not share it. He keeps a distance from formal religion, and those who know his story understand why.

He was born in the Los Angeles of 1938 to a photographer father and a schoolteacher mother. His father, it seems, had gained some notoriety for his work, and there are photographs of young Chuck with luminaries of the Hollywood smart set and even with sports stars like boxer Joe Louis. Something went wrong, though—this is the first of several unexplained secrets in the Heath story—and when Chuck was ten, his father moved the family to Hope, Idaho. His mother taught school again, and his father drove a bus and freelanced.

As often happens after a move to a new place, the Heath family was thrown in upon itself. And here is where the tensions likely arose. Chuck's mother was a devoted Christian Scientist. She believed that sin and sickness and even death were manifestations of the mind. If one simply learned to perceive the world through the *Divine Mind,* one would live free from such mortal forces. It likely seemed foolishness to a teenaged Chuck, who was not only discovering the great outdoors and finding it the only church he would ever need but also discovering his own gift for science, for decoding the wonders of nature. There was tension in the home, then, between this budding naturalist and his mystic mother. Arguments were frequent, and from this point on, young Chuck seemed intent upon escaping his parent's presence as much as possible.

He soon discovered his athletic gifts too, and, though his parents thought such pursuits were a waste of time, he chose to ride the bus fifteen miles every day to Sandpoint High School and then hitch-hike home again just so he could play nearly every sport his school offered. He found gridiron glory as a fullback behind later Green Bay Packers legend Jerry Kramer.

These were agonizing years, though. He routinely slept on friends' couches when he just couldn't face hitchhiking home. He was nearly adopted by several families of his fellow players. Everyone knew his home life was torturous and tried to help, but for a boy in high school to have no meaningful place to belong, no parents who loved him for who he was without demanding a faith he could not accept—it was, as Sarah Palin herself later wrote, "painful and lonely."

After graduation from high school and a brief season in the Army, Chuck enrolled in Columbia Basin College. Now he could give himself fully to learning the ways of nature, long his passion and his hope. He collected rocks and bones, found the insides of animals and plants a fascinating other world, and thrilled to his newly acquired knowledge of geology and the life of a cell. He was a geek, but a handsome, athletic geek whom girls liked. It was during this time that he enrolled in a college biology lab and found himself paired with that lanky beauty Sally Sheeran.

"Almighty, everlasting God, Father of our Lord Jesus Christ," the minister implores, "look with favor on your servant, Sarah, whom it has pleased you to call to this first step in the faith. Rid her of all inward blindness. Sever all snares of Satan, which heretofore bound her. Open wide for her, Lord, the door to your fatherly love. May the seal of your wisdom so penetrate her as to cast out all tainted and foul inclinations, and let in the fragrance of your lofty teachings. Thus shall she serve you gladly in your church and grow daily more perfect through Christ our Lord."

It says a great deal about Chuck and Sally Heath that after they had married—after they had brought three children into the world and begun working in their professions and coached sports and enjoyed their outdoor, adventurous lives—there was still something missing. Sandpoint simply wasn't enough. Chuck, ever the romantic, had begun reading the works of Jack London—*The Call of the Wild*, *White Fang*, and *The Sea Wolf*—and through these the great land in the north— Alaska—began calling to him. As a neighbor later reported, "The call of the wild got to him." This neighbor did not mean the London novel, but rather that mysterious draw to the raw and untamed that has lured men to Alaska for centuries. It did not hurt that Alaska was in desperate need of science teachers like Chuck, and that the school systems there were offering $6,000 a year, twice what Chuck was making in Sandpoint. With a growing family and dreams that Idaho could not contain, Chuck Heath turned to his wife and said, "Let's try it for one year and see what happens." Sally should have known better. They would never come back to Idaho again. Alaska was the land of Chuck's dreams and always would be.

It also says a great deal about Chuck and Sally Heath that they ventured north to Alaska just days after the state had been rocked by one of the worst earthquakes in history. On March 27, 1964, what became known as the Good Friday Earthquake shook Alaska at a 9.2 Richter scale magnitude for nearly five minutes. The quake was felt as far away as eight hundred miles from the epicenter.[2] Experts compared it to the 1812 New Madrid earthquake that was so powerful it caused the Mississippi River to run backward, stampeded buffalo on the prairie, and awakened President James Madison from a sound sleep in the White House. The Good Friday Earthquake did hundreds of millions dollars in damage, cost dozens of lives, and vanquished entire communities in Alaska, but even this devastation could not keep the Heath family away.

They would live first in Skagway, then in Anchorage, and finally they would be able to afford their own home in the little valley town of Wasilla. Chuck would teach sciences and coach, and Sally would do whatever paid—work in the cafeteria, serve as the school secretary, even coach some of the athletic teams.

This is what they did. Who they were is the more interesting tale.

The Heaths were determined to create an outpost of love, learning, and adventure in their snowy valley in the north. Their lives were very nearly a frontier existence, as we shall see, but their learning and their hunger to explore lifted them from mere survival. Chuck found Alaska an Elysium for scientific inquiry, and as he hunted and served as a trail guide, he collected. The Heath children would grow up in a home that might elsewhere have passed for a small natural history museum. Years after first arriving in Alaska, when their famous daughter had forced their lives into the international spotlight, the Heaths would welcome reporters who sat at their kitchen counter and marveled at the skins and pelts and mounts—dozens of them—that adorned the house. There were fossils and stuffed alligators and hoofs from some long-ago-killed game and samples of rock formations and Eskimo artifacts. The reporters had been warned. In the front yard of the Heath house stood a fifteen-foot-tall mountain of antlers, most all from game shot by Chuck Heath.

Yet what distinguished the Heath home was its elevated vision, its expectations for character and knowledge. There would come a day when Sally's spiritual search would lead her in a different direction than her husband had chosen—his conflicts with his Christian Science mother distancing him from traditional faith—and this would have to be managed. But there was complete agreement about the other essentials. Work was sacred. Everyone was expected to labor for the good of the family. Knowledge was paramount. Theirs was a home filled with books, and nearly each one was read aloud more than once. Since both Chuck and Sally were teachers, dinnertimes were often occasions of debate or discussion, which Chuck frequently began by reading from a Paul Harvey newspaper column or by quoting from a radio broadcast he had heard during the day. So intent upon the primacy of learning were Chuck and Sally that when a television finally did make its way into their home, it lived in a room over the unheated garage where a potential viewer had to have a death wish to brave the cold. Rather than what Chuck and Sally called *the boob tube*, in the warmth of the house were the poetry of Ogden Nash and Robert Service, the works of C. S. Lewis, and most of the great books of the American experience.

There was also love. It was deep, transforming, and infectious in the Heath home. When friends of the Heath children missed their school bus home, they routinely made their way to the Heaths' house. Their parents knew and understood. It was the place where strangers were always welcome, where a story was always being told, and where you merged seamlessly into the family mayhem the moment you stepped through the door. Some of those friends of the Heath children, now adults, recall that the closest thing they ever experienced to a healthy family was in Chuck and Sally's home.

And so the Heaths did it. They carved out the life they had dreamed in the frozen wilds of Alaska. They took the best of their family lines and, refusing the worst, built a family culture of courage and learning and industry and joy. And this was the family soil from which Sarah Palin grew.

Thus, the reverend father comes to an end:

> *Holy Lord, almighty Father, everlasting God, source of light and truth, I appeal to your sacred and boundless compassion on behalf of this servant of yours, Sarah. Be pleased to enlighten her by the light of your eternal wisdom. Cleanse, sanctify, and endow her with truth and knowledge. For thus will she be made ready for your grace and ever remain steadfast, never*

losing hope, never faltering in duty, never straying from sacred truth, through Christ our Lord.[3]

The service concluded, the Heath family and their near relatives walk out into the northwestern sun. It is June 7. Already there are tears, and they are not tears of joy. The Heaths' presence in Richland is not just for the sake of the baptism. They have come to say good-bye. Alaska calls to them, and they will leave in a few short days to make the nineteen-hundred-mile drive to their new home in the land of the north. Their relatives grieve, but the Heaths, particularly Chuck, cannot hide their joy at the looming adventure. Nor can they hide the sense that they will be changed by their new land, that somehow they will become one with it, and that it will become mystically intertwined with their destiny in ways they could never imagine.

In a matter of few days then, attended by the tears of their loved ones, the Heath family step toward the great land of their dreams.

Chapter 2

PROFILE: THE GREAT LAND

Some of the hardiest people in the society were drawn to bush Alaska in search of a sense of release—of a life that remembered the past. The Alaskan wild was, as advertised, the last frontier.[1]

—JOHN MCPHEE
Coming Into the Country

I T WAS EMINENT AMERICAN HISTORIAN DAVID MCCULLOUGH who wrote, "If character is destiny, so too, I believe, is terrain."[2] McCullough certainly meant, at least in the traditional sense, that land fashions history and therefore fashions destiny nearly as much as men do. It is the commander's battle for the high ground or the settler's struggle with the unending prairie or the explorer's assault on unyielding mountains that is the stuff of history. There is no human endeavor unfashioned by the contours and demands of the land, and so there is no portion of the human story in which geography does not feature in the tale. Yes, terrain, in its most physical and stark sense, is destiny.

Yet McCullough may also have intended to speak of the inner impact of terrain. In the same way that character exerts itself on the soul toward noble ends, terrain shapes the soul as well. The land upon which we live fashions us not just by its outer insistences but also by what it comes to symbolize in our hearts and minds, by the pull that it exerts on our inner life. Mountains can become icons of longing unfulfilled, vast expanses can reinforce a passion for freedom, and a man's struggle for mastery of the land can become a metaphor for his sense of contending for his calling—or contending with his God. Terrain is destiny in this sense too—it chisels and informs the inner man.

It is foolishness, then, to try to understand notable lives without understanding the land in which they lived and invested themselves. True, many live rootless, disconnected lives without the grounding that comes from belonging to a place. Yet what would Churchill have been without the downs of Kent or Washington without the dense forests of Northern Virginia? Would we have had Lincoln without the plains of Illinois? Or Burns without the highlands of Scotland? Even those who later chose a terrain different from that of their birth often did so because their new land fit the contours of their inner life. Ronald Reagan grew up barely a hundred miles from Chicago, but he chose a saddle, a cowboy hat, and a ranch in California because it better suited the inner vision and perhaps the political philosophy of his life. McCullough was right in this sense too—terrain both makes and reveals the man or the woman.

By the time she became John McCain's running mate in the fall of 2008, Sarah Palin had spent more than four decades of her life in Alaska. She had been carried there shortly after her birth and had grown up fully connected to its landscape, its lore, its lessons, and its punishments. She had been taught to love it and had absorbed its meaning as deeply as any. Indeed, she had lived in a type of Alaskan isolation and so did not know how much she had been shaped by her native land and how odd it would all seem to an unknowing and suspicious outer world.

The tensions became obvious on the campaign trail. Staffers knew early on that something was wrong. Palin was preoccupied with polls and surveys from back home and agonized over how the campaign was playing among "her people." She was heard to complain that she would trade all the fancy food in the campaign hotel suites and buses for one good bowl of moose chili. She came into conflict with McCain's senior staffers because she wanted to campaign in Michigan, a state that Republican strategists had already decided was solidly in Democrat hands. Palin felt that the people of Michigan were like her tribe back home—blue collar, largely Northern European by heritage, shaped by brutal winters and life near the sea. In other words, Michigan was Alaska in the Lower 48, and Palin wanted to be there. Before long staffers began to understand: Palin was homesick, and in a way that is hard to fully comprehend for those who have never completely belonged to a portion of the earth.

And belonging to Alaska is no light experience. Its sheer size threatens to overwhelm. Alaska is some 570,374 square miles, which means it is equal to one-fifth of the Lower 48 states and larger than most of the nations of the world. On this massive tract of land live not even 700,000 people, only slightly more than the number who live in the less than 70 square miles of Washington DC. It means that there is almost a square mile of Alaska for every Alaskan, the perfect ratio for the independent, the freedom loving, the dreamers, and the curmudgeon.

It is the wildness, though, that is the great mystery and lure. Sarah Palin was born when Alaska had been a state for only five years. The land then was frontier in every sense. There were men in those days who lived, dressed, and believed as men had for centuries in that frozen paradise. Men with long beards and hand-fashioned clothes still disappeared into the mountains and returned months later with pack animals near to collapse from the weight of pelts and furs. Eskimo villages still hunted whales from sealskin canoes, and towns at the base of mountains looked like Dodge City of the Old West transplanted and encased in snow.

It is hard for Americans from the Lower 48—part of that remote world Alaskans call *outside*—to understand. Alaska can be as high-tech and contemporary as any state. In fact, there are more airplane pilots in Alaska as a percentage of population than any other place in the world. Yet the huge distances and the hold of the land on the soul can insulate and make many Alaskans anachronisms. Even some of the political challenges of modern Alaska are rooted in centuries-old issues barely comprehensible elsewhere in the United States. A visitor to Anchorage in March of 2010 would have heard news reports that the State Department of Education had granted alternative test dates to the children of a remote band of religious Russians. Called the *Old Believers*, this group of ultraconservative Russian Orthodox Christians split from the rest of Russian Ortho-doxy over theological matters that arose in the 1600s. Yet, today, in Alaska, these obscure issues and their implications for the state's educational calendar become the stuff of public policy. It is in Alaska as it is in no other state.

The portion of Alaska in which Sarah Palin would grow up and first spread her political wings was a particularly isolated region with a particularly unusual history. Called the *Matanuska-Susitna Valley—Mat-Su* by locals—this fertile land of stunning vistas lies between the Talkeetna and Chugach mountains just forty-five minutes north of Anchorage. Poor roads and rugged terrain made the trip from the Mat-Su to Anchorage nearly a day's journey for most of its inhabited history, and this only deepened the cultural isolation of the region.

It would be an exaggeration to say that Sarah Palin grew up on the American frontier. This would sound like the claims of mythmakers and hagiographers. Still, culturally and practically it is not far from the truth. Palin's hometown of Wasilla, at the heart of the Mat-Su Valley, was founded in 1917, but a photograph from 1947 shows the village to be barely a handful of rough-hewn shacks thirty years later. This was less than two decades before Palin's family arrived.

What growth did come resulted from the policies of a U.S. government based nearly four thousand miles away. During the Great Depression of the 1930s, New Deal strategists sought to encourage agriculture in Alaska—which had never thrived—and rescue families from the economic suffering in the Midwest by transplanting farmers from Wisconsin, Minnesota, and Michigan to the Mat-Su Valley. Each farmer was promised land for as little as five dollars an acre, free transportation from the Lower 48, and housing. It was a dream come true for many a suffering Midwestern family, particularly since the long Alaskan days and lack of crop-damaging pests seemed to promise success. There was also the appeal of escaping the devastating dust bowl conditions that plagued middle America. Carried aloft by such hopes, hundreds of *colonists* went north.

Typically, there had been no preparation. As late as 1935, no permanent housing existed, and the tracts of land promised to each farmer were just so many lines on a survey map. Still, in true pioneer fashion, these homesteaders dug in. Rains destroyed their crops, soil quality proved uneven, and fights over land ensued. Most farmers found that even forty acres was not nearly enough on which to survive. But they stayed. And labored. And hoped.

Their struggles became part of the Wasilla and Mat-Su Valley culture. When Sarah Palin's future pastor Paul Riley arrived as an eager, young Assembly of God preacher in the 1950s—but a few years before Palin's family first drove into town—he discovered a society and lived a lifestyle closer to that which Abraham Lincoln would have known than to those who lived in the Lower 48 at the time.

Wasilla was a community of some thirty homes so spread out into the woods and contours of the valley that there really was no town to speak of. A community hall, service station, roadhouse, and depot were all that signaled civilization. Riley was given permission to hold church services in the community center, but only if he chopped his own firewood to heat the place. He lived in a tiny house with no running water, one light bulb, and cardboard dividers between *rooms*. A wood stove heated well, but it meant even more wood chopping for the young pastor. Fortunately, in the astonishingly fertile valley, an acre and a half of land yielded twelve tons of potatoes, and so Riley and his wife never lacked for food.

Everything lagged decades behind the rest of the world. Though it was now the mid-1960s, radio was the primary source of news, the few tiny black-and-white televisions little more than conversation pieces. Most homes had outhouses, had no electricity, burned wood for heat, and used water pumped from a well. Many a family simply sent one of its members to the local creek for water. The staples were potatoes, moose meat, fish, and a type of coffee so thick and pungent that Riley winces at the memory to this day. Roads were mud or gravel. Many an old timer remembers mainly the smell of creosote, which was common among a people living near fires and which made everything from hair to clothing to the very walls reek of *burnt*.

Loneliness was an insidious enemy. Men were often away for weeks at a time working in Anchorage or hunting, and women were left in the dark, frigid Alaskan outback to fend for themselves. More than one wife in Wasilla neared insanity because of the isolation and the fear. The drive to Anchorage was more than three hours in length in those days, wound through the mountains, and was treacherous. Few attempted it unless necessary, thus deepening the sense of seclusion and, often, the despair.

Still, as frontier people have for centuries, Paul Riley and his companions in the Mat-Su Valley learned to find strength and joy in each other. Hospitality and generosity turned frozen outposts into loving communities. Skills were shared. There was the woman who knew how to decorate cakes and the mother who cut hair in her kitchen and the man who would teach anyone who sat still long enough how to fix a pump. And every occasion became an opportunity to have that second cup of coffee, tell a story, and share a meaningful moment.

In times of death the community rallied. Pastor Riley remembers that when a man died, he was put in the freezer. This was no callous disregard. It took time to dig a grave in the frozen ground and time to build the coffin by hand. Once both were prepared, the body of the deceased was usually put in Riley's station wagon and taken to the graveside. People lived close to the earth and close to each other. It was no different when a member of the community died. Returning a body to the earth and the soul to God was part of what a caring community did. This and a thousand deeds like it made life in the frozen wilds tolerable. And this was true late in the 1960s, when most Americans assumed such lifestyles had passed away with the western frontier.

It was in this world that Sarah Palin grew up. She did not live a *Little House on the Prairie* existence, but she lived one close to it, and it has done much to shape who she is. She stacked firewood nearly every day of her childhood—not to create an attractive fire in an otherwise centrally heated house, but because the family would freeze to death without a fire. She participated in the family hunting experiences not just for sport but because the family needed the meat. She knew men who froze to death in the mountains, and she visited Eskimo villages that were Catholic or Presbyterian simply because pioneering missionaries from those faiths got there first. And always she felt protected and summoned by the mountains, and as she took them in, she wondered about that faraway world *outside*.

That world would barely understand hers. In *Going Rogue* she tells a cute story that is probably intended to affirm that she is a lady despite all the blustery hunter gal rhetoric. It seems one morning before school she went hunting with her father. They shot a moose, and as her dad cleaned the animal, he tried to hand Sarah the just-extracted eyeballs. Sarah winced, shook her head, and her understanding father put the steaming moose eyeballs elsewhere.

Palin's point is her squeamishness at the eyeballs. What goes without comment is the rest of the experience. She lived in a culture where getting out of a warm bed at three or four in the morning to go hunting was normal. It wasn't even unusual on a school day. Because she is used to the experience, Sarah also does not comment on the great ordeal of cleaning a moose. To gut and clean an animal of such size requires exceptional strength and skill and yields huge amounts of blood, dozens of pounds of entrails, and often nauseating smells. Sarah was used to all of it. It was part of her world, in natural flow with the rest of her life. She would traipse off to school hours later and play basketball when classes were done and never think it strange that she had begun her day so early, so far from the experience of an average American girl or so much in what is traditionally regarded as a man's world. It all seemed normal because it was the only life Sarah Palin knew, and she would not truly understand how odd it all was to most Americans until she ran for the vice presidency of the United States.

By then Alaska had marked her. It had made her confident in the work of her hands, respectful of tradition, and devoted to community. She had absorbed, as though through her pores, that belonging to the land was preferable to never having roots, that having place among a people meant a life worth living. She had become a *Sourdough*, that old settler term for someone who had been in the land a long time. Once she and her family had been *Cheechakos*, the Chinook Indian term for newcomers to the north, but now they belonged. They had bled and built and invested. Now Alaska was theirs.

It was something the merely political and the unlanded would never understand. And so they mocked and jeered when she spoke of her love for her place on the earth and of what Alaska had taught her. For those who would listen, though, the poetry was inescapable, the wisdom seeping through the odes to her native land. This was perhaps most grandly on display when she left the job she loved the most and perhaps should never have aspired beyond. In her final speech as governor, on July 26, 2009, she threw a verbal bouquet to the terrain that held her soul in its loving grip.

> And getting up here, I say it is the best road trip in America, soaring through nature's finest show. Denali, the great one, soaring under the midnight sun. And then the extremes. In the winter time it's the frozen road that is competing with the view of the ice-fogged frigid beauty. The cold though: Doesn't it split the Cheechakos from the Sourdoughs? And then in the summertime, such extreme summertime, about a hundred and fifty degrees hotter than just some months ago, than just months from now, with fireweed blooming along the frost heaves and merciless rivers that are rushing and carving and reminding us that here, Mother Nature wins. It is as throughout all Alaska, that big wild good life teeming along the road that is north to the future.[3]

It is this love of land, rootedness, and belonging that have defined Palin and made her much of what she is. Outsiders may never fully comprehend it, but she will likely never stop trying to help them understand. When the 2008 campaign was done, and she had written *Going Rogue*, one of the first projects she pursued was a cable television series that portrayed the glories of Alaska to the Lower 48 via cable television. This was in keeping with a mission of her life: to impress the values and the heritage of her native state on the collective soul of the rest of America. This, she believes, will be a healing, an elevating experience for her second home—the United States.

Chapter 3

WARRIOR RISING

I learned this, at least, by my experiment; that if one advances confidently in the direction of his dreams, and endeavors to live the life which he has imagined, he will meet with a success unexpected in common hours.[1]
—HENRY DAVID THOREAU
Walden

We REMEMBER OUR LIVES IN SNAPSHOTS. PSYCHOLOGISTS tell us that this is because our inner being is ever arranging the scenes of our history according to a narrative of the mind. The scenes that fit this narrative live vividly in our imaginations, and we recall them as if they occurred in tight succession, though years might actually have separated each one. We tend to perceive our memories in much the same way we might perceive a range of mountains. Viewed from a certain perspective, each mountain seems to stand right beside the next, though actually miles separate them. To condense and define in this way is human. We naturally arrange to gain perspective, to put what we know in a story. In fact, this yearning for narrative helps us make sense of what we know and to draw from it the meaning it is intended to have for our lives.

There is a narrative that emerges early in the life of Sarah Palin.

It is confirmed by the surviving snapshots of her life, and it carries through to the personality we see on our national stage today. This narrative centers upon the strong-willed, even combative, personality that arose in young Sarah during her formative years. It seems to be a gift of nature rather than nurture. Though it may have found its source in her father's determined, nonconformist personality, there is little of it at work in the rest of Sarah's family. This insistent manner may have been a blessing of her unique destiny, but it would not always be welcomed by those around her, and it would require tempering before it would serve her well.

Sarah relates the first snapshot of this unfolding narrative in the opening pages of *Going Rogue*. It occurred in Skagway one day when she was only four and was walking the elevated wooden sidewalks of that rustic town. Typically, she found herself wondering at the laws of physics and why they should uniquely apply to her.

> I got to thinking: I had seen eagles and dragonflies and ptarmigan fly, but I had never seen a person fly. That didn't make sense to me. Hadn't anyone ever tried it before? Why couldn't someone just propel herself up into the air and get it done?
>
> I stopped and looked up at the summer sky, then down at the dirt road below. Then I simply jumped. I didn't care who might see me. I wanted to fly more than I worried about what I looked like. My knees took most of the impact, and I scraped them both.[2]

It is a cute childhood story, and alone it would signal little, but there is another, and it seems to confirm the emerging pattern. At about the same time, Palin remembers "arguing with the nun who taught catechism and tried to teach me to write the letter *E*. It seemed a naked letter to me, so I was determined to reinvent it. I insisted she let me improve it with at least a few more horizontal lines."[3]

This insistence, this stubbornness, became the manner of her life. Years later, when Sarah was governor of Alaska, her father told those who asked him to intercede with her on their behalf, "I gave up on trying to get her to do anything she didn't want to do back when she was two." Her brother confirmed this strain in her nature. "She never lost an argument," he said, "and would never, no matter what, back down when she knew she was right. Not just with me or the other kids, but with Mom and Dad too."[4]

We should merge this understanding of her nature with another. Sarah was bookish and introverted. She kept to herself, and friends from her early years often thought that she hid somewhat behind the huge glasses on her nose and the book in her hand. She was undoubtedly digging a deep well through her reading and the daydreams it inspired, but still she could roar out of these reveries in fiery defense of what she believed to be true.

The loner in her was drawn out in her early teen years by a family activity that provides another snapshot in the narrative of her life. This was in the mid-1970s, and jogging had become an American craze. The popularity of the sport rose on the fame of a handful of new stars. Frank Shorter's victory in the men's marathon at the tragedy-scarred 1972 Munich Olympic Games had made him an instant celebrity. Four years later, long-distance runner Steve Prefontaine attained rock star status simply by running longer and faster than anyone else ever had. And implausibly for the disco-era, Jim Fixx's tome, *The Complete Book of Running*, owned the top spot on the *New York Times* nonfiction list for eleven straight weeks in 1977.

Chuck Heath became caught up in the running craze and took his family with him. Perhaps it was the challenge that appealed: the lung-exploding, agonizing pursuit of greater distance and harder paths. It may too have been the quiet and the self-possession of a long-distance, Alaska run. Whatever the appeal, the whole family bought in. Even Sally, never an athlete, trained and finished marathons at her husband's side. This was an exceptional feat, for Chuck became such a good runner that he finished the Boston Marathon twice.

Sarah seemed to absorb the passion for running as deeply as any. Chuck often acknowledged that Sarah was his least athletically gifted child. She was the bookworm, the brain. Her siblings could already envision her as a librarian or an English teacher. But there was something about the run and how it gave her a reason to master herself, body and soul, that called to her.

It was the great Czech marathoner from the 1950s, Emil Zapotek, who once observed, "It's at the borders of pain and suffering that the men are separated from the boys."[5] This was likely what drew Sarah to the sport. The introvert in her liked that running is about an inner dialogue, that it is an argument between body and mind. A cross-country runner needs above all else the capacity to push herself beyond her perceived limits. To keep going when every muscle fiber screams for rest and the lungs burn from cold. To hit what distance runners call *the wall* and then press through. Of this, Zapotek once said, "If you want to win something, run the 100 meters. If you want to experience something, run a marathon."[6]

Here we find a key to Palin's character. Though she thrives on devotion to family, friends, and tribe, she is at heart a loner. She works from the inside out, draws from an inner flame of inspiration that few understand but many admire. It is what made a woman physically unsuited for long-distance running into a woman who prizes her running achievement almost on equal terms with all else she has accomplished. It is touching to read her boast in *Going Rogue* that as a state governor and mother of four, she once broke the four-hour barrier in a local marathon. This is because she likes Zapotek's "borders of pain and suffering." She likes challenging herself, proving herself against the world and her inner image of what she can be. Running gave her rich inner life—that life that made her such a contented introvert—a means to exert herself triumphantly over her external world.

These first two snapshots are of Sarah within herself, of Sarah self-contained. It would require another snapshot-worthy scene—and yet another sport—to temper her hardheadedness and to awaken the gift for leadership that would ever after define her days.

She has said, "Everything I ever needed to know, I learned on the basketball court."[7] Those who knew her in her early teens would certainly have been surprised that this would one day be so. She had few of the gifts that make for greatness on the court. She was not tall. She was not swift. She was not exceptionally graceful. She had little of the court sense that makes for great players. What she did have—and this is a hallmark of her life—was *heart*. She could outhustle and outwork most other players, and this is what gave her the career that came to mean so much.

In 1980, her sophomore year in high school, Sarah played on the Wasilla High School junior varsity team with the rest of her classmates. That year she watched with vicarious excitement and a twinge of envy as her older, taller sister, Heather, helped take the Wasilla varsity team to the state championship game as a standout junior player. The Warriors lost that game, but hopes in the community were high that with returning starters like Heather Heath, the team was positioned to make another run at a state title: "We'll get 'em next year!"

Sarah harbored some lofty aspirations of her own. The competitive edge she had acquired through her running made her expect not only to suit up with the varsity team, but also to enjoy a large amount of court time as well. Yet, as the new season unfolded, these hopes were quickly dashed. Wasilla's coach, Don Teeguarden, had arrived at a plan for the season, and it didn't include much playing time for Sarah or her good friend and fellow junior, Michelle Carney. It was a blow to her ambitious soul. Sarah chafed on the practice squad and, desperate to change a situation she viewed as unjust, launched an appeal.

All arguments fell on deaf ears. Coach Teeguarden was unmoved.

That avenue failing, Sarah and her friend besieged the assistant coach, Cordell Randall, and asked him to intercede. Randall promised to talk to Teeguarden about the matter and did—though not as the girls had envisioned.

Randall went to Teeguarden and suggested that if Carney and the younger Heath were so desperate to play, they could be moved back down to the JV squad, which he coached. There they would start every game. Teeguarden liked the idea. There was a strategic logic to the move in that it gave two players who were going to be needed the following year—a rebuilding year by most expectations—some valuable playing experience, certainly much more than they would enjoy on the varsity squad. The decision carried the added advantage of getting the girls off his back and sending a pointed message to the others about challenging their coach's decisions.

It was a lesson not lost on Sarah. Although initially humiliated and angered by what was the high school equivalent of being sent down to the minor leagues, she gave herself to her new role and played her heart out. Her coach was impressed, both by her playing and by her newly tempered attitude. As a star on the JV team, her skills sharpened, her confidence soared, and she became a valued leader.

At the end of that season, the Wasilla varsity girls found themselves playing for the state championship for the second consecutive year. And for a second time, Sarah, though allowed to suit up for the game, was stuck helplessly on the sidelines watching her friends go into battle. That year the Lady Warriors lost a heartbreaker by a single basket.

The 1981–1982 school year finally brought Sarah her chance to play. She was desperate for practices to begin. Yet when they did, she discovered that Coach Teeguarden—a man with a gift for assessing talent and building strategies around it—had determined a season game plan that left her in yet another vastly different role from the one she had imagined.

In Teeguarden's strategic plan, Sarah's primary role would be defensive. She would press the opposing team's ball handler—using her outstanding conditioning and natural tenaciousness to attack, attack, attack. On offense, her role was simple: she was to patiently and methodically work the ball in to one of two bigger girls maneuvering for position near the basket for a high-percentage, close-range shot. Since in those days there was no shot clock limiting how long a team could control the ball, Teeguarden's strategy was brilliant and fit his team's skill perfectly. It did not produce glamorous basketball, and it offered no opportunity for Sarah to follow in her older sister's footsteps as an offensive star, but Don Teeguarden believed it was a winning strategy given the personnel he had.

The plan was a blow to Sarah. Yet, ever the team player, she soon settled into her assigned game. And it worked. For an opponent, trying to move the ball up the court with Sarah defending was akin to dribbling past a buzz saw crossed with a whirling dervish. Her cross-country running had given her a conditioning edge over other players, and her temperament made her relentlessly aggressive. Opposing players were often stunned from the first moments of the game and seldom recovered themselves. Sarah's only challenge was learning to stay out of foul trouble. Then too there was the disappointment of her limited offensive possibilities. Most of her scoring came at the free throw line after she was fouled while handling the ball.

Sarah and two other senior girls were named co-captains and, as the season progressed, it became clear to all that Coach Teeguarden's strategy was a sound one. The team only lost a few games in the regular season, but one of them was a forty-point drubbing at the hands of big East Anchorage High. As in the previous two years, the Warriors successfully fought their way through the regional tournament at the end of the season. As regional champs, they qualified to participate in the state tournament—earning a shot at the championship glory that had just eluded the previous two Wasilla squads.

In one of the final games of the regional tournament, Sarah landed awkwardly on an ankle, rolled it severely, and came up hobbling. At that point her season should have been over, but she insisted on playing through the pain, and this determination in turn set up one of the defining snapshots of her life.

In the championship game against Anchorage Service High, a school more than three times the size of Wasilla High, the Warriors held a slim lead throughout most of the first half. Shortly after the start of the second half, it became clear to Teeguarden that Sarah's lateral movement on the injured ankle was badly compromised, that the opposing coach had noticed it, and that they were adjusting their strategy to exploit this vulnerability in the Warrior defense. Service started closing the gap.

Reluctantly, Teeguarden signaled a substitute and sent Sarah to the bench. It was a crushing disappointment, but she understood. She certainly didn't want to be responsible for her teammates blowing their big chance. Part of her really believed, though, that if she could stay out there in the battle, she could just *run through it*. It is what she had always done on those lonely, painful long-distance runs.

With about a minute left to play in the game, Wasilla was barely holding on to a four-point lead when Sarah heard her coach bark her name. She was being put back in. Sarah checked in at the scorer's table, limped back out onto the floor, took an inbound pass from her teammate, and gamely dribbled the ball down the court as best she could. The Service High girls, running out of time and needing two baskets to tie, aggressively went after the ball and were called for a foul. Sarah hobbled to the free throw line for a "one-and-one," meaning that if she made the first shot, she would get a second attempt.

Her first effort swished and increased the Warriors lead to an insurmountable five points. She missed the second free throw, but it didn't matter. As it turned out, her shot—her only point of the evening—was the last one of the game. Wasilla High had won the championship against one of the largest schools in Alaska. It is a victory still recounted on the streets of Wasilla to this day.

These three snapshots are images of emerging character that have become part of the defining narrative of Palin's life. Sarah headstrong and certain. Sarah digging deep into her extensive inner world to become the runner of her dreams, to prevent biology from becoming destiny. Sarah surmounting the pain and the disappointment to serve her team's call. Sarah in pursuit of victory. Sarah, tempered, rising again. Sarah neither the best nor the most gifted, showing how determination alone can carry the day.

These are the images. This is the narrative. In this way the mountains are perceived. And from the narrative that these memories are often summoned to support, we gain insight into the woman Sarah Palin believes herself to be.

Chapter 4

THE TURNING

If we find ourselves with a desire that nothing in this world can satisfy, the most probable explanation is that we were made for another world.

—C. S. LEWIS
Mere Christianity

THERE WAS A TIME IN AMERICAN SOCIETY WHEN DISCUSSING one's religion was considered taboo. The mere mention of religion or politics in polite company was met with discomfort, and all because these topics were thought too divisive for those who wished cohesion at all costs.

Our world has changed. Religion is at the heart of some of our greatest global crises: terrorism, genocide, and even the threat of nuclear war. Political leaders have concealed their intentions behind pious mush, and this has left the electorate more cynical, less willing to be bought off politically with religious sentiment rather than clearly explained theological beliefs. There is also the rise of a new breed of young voters who are impatient with bluster and who want political leaders to cut to the chase, to explain exactly what they believe and what it will mean for the people. Each of these has made Americans insistent upon open discussion of the faiths that will shape their public lives.

This insistence is particularly directed at politicians who root their politics in religious soil, and Sarah Palin is unquestionably among this tribe.

When she was summoned to be McCain's running mate and an aide commented that she was particularly calm in the midst of the storm, she explained simply, "It's God's plan."[1] This confidence sprang from a strong sense of divine predetermination, from a belief that God orchestrates human lives according to His will: "I always subscribed to concepts like Providence and purpose, that people aren't just random collections of molecules stumbling aimlessly through history. I believed—and still do—that each person has a destiny, a reason for being."[2] Palin believes that the same God who predetermined her life also gave it meaning, and that this meaning extends even to her politics, as we shall see.

This faith in a destiny-weaving God first took root in Palin's life as the result of her mother's spiritual search. Sally Heath had been raised in an Irish Catholic home and insisted upon devotion to this same faith when she had a family of her own. Her children would spend their early years in the catechisms and confirmations that the Roman Catholic Church expected of her young, and all the Heaths would accept this as a matter of course. Yet by the time Sally found herself putting down roots in Wasilla, she had begun to feel uneasy about her religious life.

As she later explained it, she had made church a part of her family's life more out of an inherited cultural habit than out of any meaningful conviction. With the passing of years, she came to see that she had never really owned Catholicism for herself. This created a crisis. She knew she was a *good person*, but in her private moments she did not feel *whole*, did not feel the connection to God that religion is supposed to be about. She found herself hungering for more.

There followed a progression, a layering of experiences, as there often is in the journey to new faith. A co-worker in the school cafeteria invited Sally to attend her church. She agreed, and the next Sunday she herded her children to a small, independent Bible church called Church in the Wildwood. It was an odd experience for Sally. When she returned home and Chuck asked how it went, she replied, "It was nice, I guess, but they sure talk about Jesus a lot."

Then there was that Easter Sunday service at the local Roman Catholic church in Wasilla during which the priest read those words that stirred Sally's soul. They were the words of Jesus in the third chapter of the Book of Revelation, and Sally would never forget them: "I know your works: you are neither cold nor hot. Would that you were cold or hot! So, because you are lukewarm, and neither cold nor hot, I will spew you out of my mouth."[3] The thought that a lackadaisical Christian could sicken the Blessed Savior stunned Sally, and she began to wonder if she might be among those whom Jesus was rebuking in this astonishing passage.

Punctuating both of these experiences was a moment that occurred a few weeks later when Sally attended a women's meeting at Abbott Loop Community Church in Anchorage. She had never felt anything like it. The women who gathered had sung songs of deep spiritual passion, songs that expressed a longing for intimacy with God. Sally had been moved and was equally stirred by the teaching, which was simple and warm and came from the Bible as though intended for her alone. And when the message was done, there was an invitation for those who wanted to "receive Christ as their personal Savior." Sally had responded—and she knew it had left her changed.

Still, she was confused. What was happening to her? Why was this unfamiliar brand of Christianity so different from her Catholic faith? To get answers, she first sought out the Presbyterian minister at the church where she was working part-time. Sally carefully described what had happened to her and the change she was sure was taking place. The minister merely shrugged and dismissed the whole experience as meaningless emotionalism. Frustrated, Sally then made an appointment with the priest at her Catholic church. Sally again described what she had seen. The priest seemed concerned: "I've heard about this kind of thing happening to people. It's going around. You don't want to have anything to do with it."

None of this satisfied. Sally was too convinced that something significant was happening to her. She expressed her frustration to a friend. "You should go talk to Paul Riley," the friend insisted. "He'll be able to explain this to you." The suggestion gave Sally hope. She knew of Riley, knew that he had founded the local Assembly of God church in the early 1950s and that he was one of the most respected Christian leaders in the area. She was sure he would have the answers.

Riley was a tall, gentle, kind-faced man whose manner was comforting to Sally the day she met with him. As she chaotically poured out her experiences and her confusion, Riley listened quietly, his large, muscular hands folded. Finally, he leaned forward, opened his Bible, and explained what he knew the eager woman before him had experienced. He used the term *new birth* and showed Sally the passage in the third chapter of John's Gospel in which Jesus says, "Truly, truly, I say to you, unless one is born of water and the Spirit, he cannot enter into the kingdom of God....You must be born again."[4] Riley used words like *surrender* and *transformation*. He explained about the possibility of a relationship with Jesus, an idea that had stirred Sally's heart when she heard about it once before, but Pastor Riley spoke in such gentle, understandable terms that Sally's heart was set at ease. She came to understand what it meant to be *saved*, and she realized that this is what had happened to her at that women's meeting months before.

Before Sally left her meeting with Riley, she knew that this man was to be her new pastor, that Wasilla Assembly of God was her new church home. And she knew that she would raise her children in a new way, with a faith that was personal and transforming, and that she hoped would define them all their days. And all of this was true because Sally Heath had just learned she was born again.

It was this awakening in Sally Heath's life that in turn landed her daughter Sarah in the youth ministry at Wasilla Assembly of God. It would become the nursery of Sarah's sense of calling, the seedbed of her vision for a life of political impact. Indeed, there is a direct connection between Sarah's life in the youth ministry of Wasilla Assembly and her emergence at John's McCain's side on the national stage in 2008.

When the Heath children joined their new youth group, it was already a gathering of some twenty-five teens under the direction of Ted Boatsman, a young, no-frills kind of youth leader who believed in teaching biblical truth unsparingly and leaving the results to God. On Wednesday nights while the adults met in the main sanctuary, the youth would meet in the basement below. There would be singing, some sharing of needs for prayer, and then Boatsman would teach the truth of God. There was no video screen, no entertainment passing itself off as ministry. Boatsman taught the youth much as he might teach adults, with depth, with learning, and with a sense of urgency that he felt countered the immoral pull of his unraveling generation. There would be prayer after the teaching and a moment set aside for the kids to respond. Then, when the Scriptures had been honored, and only then, it was time to discuss plans for the ice skating and the retreats and the basketball games that made the group fun.

Boatsman remembers Sarah as most do during her early life: as the quiet, bespectacled girl in the back. She was one of the *Heath kids* to him, and though she seemed to enjoy the group and gave evidence of a deepening faith, she did not distinguish herself in any meaningful way. That day would come, though, and it would be, in part, a result of a choice Sarah made—one that would redefine the spiritual life of her entire family.

In 1964, the Alaska Assemblies of God bought some lakefront land in the heart of the Mat-Su Valley and established the Little Beaver Camp and Retreat Center. With this camp less than half an hour's drive from its front door, Wasilla Assembly was positioned to take great advantage of the facility. And it did. For Sarah Heath, her siblings, and her friends, one of the highlights of each summer was the church's weeklong youth camp. There they participated in a variety of sports and outdoor activities by day with a few classes and Bible study sessions shoehorned in between. At night, they sat in full evangelistic crusade-type services in the chapel and had more intimate, late-night devotionals in their cabins with their friends.

These camp experiences were filled with spiritual intensity and passion. The teens who attended were called to commit their lives to Jesus Christ, to *receive him as Savior and Lord.* They were told that they had a destiny that could only be fulfilled by yielding to the divine rights of Jesus Christ as King. There would be conversions and tears, late-night prayer sessions, and friendships forged to last a lifetime. So defining were these lakeside weeks that Boatsman's teens would recall them years later as turning points in their lives.

Because this was an Assemblies of God camp, there was also a strong emphasis on another transformational spiritual experience: the baptism of the Holy Spirit. The official Web site of the American Assemblies of God explains the experience in this way:

> The Baptism in the Holy Spirit is a vital experience of the Christian life. It is a special work of the Spirit beyond salvation. On the Day of Pentecost, disciples who had already made a decision to follow Jesus "were filled with the Holy Spirit and began to speak in other tongues" (Acts 2:4). Paul asked the Ephesian disciples if they had received the Holy Spirit, after which "the

Holy Spirit came on them, and they spoke in tongues" (Acts 19:2). New Testament believers were constantly challenged to be filled with the Spirit (Acts 1:4, 5; Ephesians 5:18). The Assemblies of God is committed to the baptism in the Holy Spirit because the experience is such an important focus of New Testament Christianity.[5]

The young people at Little Beaver Camp were encouraged to receive the baptism in the Holy Spirit, but they were also taught that it should come only after the born-again experience. This, in turn, was signified by baptism in water.

Such teaching forced a decision upon the Heaths. Sarah had already made what Billy Graham had termed "a decision for Christ." She was eager to be baptized. Sally and the other children had also made *professions of faith*, but they had only been christened in the Roman Catholic Church. None had been baptized in water as their new church taught them to do. There was discussion, some debate, and soon it was decided that all of the Heaths but Chuck would be baptized along with Sarah.

The time has come. Pastor Paul Riley stands waist deep in the chilly, blue-green waters of Little Beaver Lake in a pair of rubber fishing waders. While the people being baptized that day would be in and out of the water quickly, Paul will be standing out there until all the candidates for baptism receive ministry. Hypothermia is a threat, but this pastor has been here before, and he is ready.

A crowd quietly gathers in a crescent shape along the shoreline, where a colorful fleet of canoes and kayaks lies ready for another busy day. In the hush of the moment, those assembled can hear the wind whooshing in the tall birch and spruce that surround the lake and the occasional laugh of a loon skipping across the glass-flat water. On the far end, a bald eagle swoops low over the lake. And in the distance, the tops of the mountains that frame the famed Hatcher Pass, jutting almost a mile into the clear blue sky, still sport a light dusting of white snow. The air smells clean and earthy—of evergreen, moss, and wildflowers.

It is Sarah's turn. She has been waiting quietly in the line of praying, hopeful people about to be baptized, but now she wades out to meet her pastor. Riley stands facing the crowd on the shore and positions Sarah in profile before him. Placing one hand on her back and raising the other to heaven, he says, "Sarah Heath, because of your profession of faith in Jesus Christ as Savior and Lord, it is my privilege to baptize you, my sister, in the name of the Father, the Son, and the Holy Ghost."

Sarah pinches her nose, and Riley lowers her gently backward into the clear water until she is completely submerged. Then he quickly lifts her out again. She wipes the cold water from her face, blinks her eyes clear, and smiles. She has given her life to God.

It would prove essential to Sarah Palin becoming the woman we know today that shortly after her baptism, a young, brash youth minister named Theron Horne replaced Ted Boatsman at Wasilla Assembly of God. In 1979, Horne was a recent graduate of the Assembly of God affiliated North Central Bible College in Minneapolis, and he was looking for a place to serve. As one of the brightest stars of his graduating class, Horne came to the attention of Pastor Paul Riley, was interviewed, accepted, and soon found himself on the way to Wasilla, Alaska, to shape lives for God.

Horne arrived in the sleepy valley town with burning ideas about how ministry to the young should be done. He was convinced that in an increasingly secular culture, churches often surrendered to the temptation to withdraw from the broader life of the community into a type of comfortable religious ghetto. This was their mistake, he believed. He had read the early church fathers and had been stirred by their insistence that the early church engage Roman culture and serve the hurting so as to win society to their message. This they did, Horne argued passionately, despite systematic persecution, despite living in a culture at odds with everything they believed. Nevertheless, these early Christians were faithful and won much of the Roman world to their God.

Horne believed that this was a lesson for Christians living in what some called *post-Christian America*. He was convinced that modern believers had compartmentalized their faith—walling it off from their work and their public lives. Horne believed that the modern church needed to learn some lessons from the founding generations of the faith.

When he arrived in Wasilla, Horne immediately went to work creating a core group of dedicated teens, some fifteen in all, and among these were several Heath children. He wanted them to lead the way in breaking out of a narrow church culture and in penetrating and impacting the broader community. For Horne, this *community* meant largely Wasilla High. Leading by example, he began having lunch at the school cafeteria to get to know the students. He made sure to reach beyond the kids from Wasilla Assembly to those who were troubled, hurting, or heading down a destructive path. Soon these students started attending Horne's Wednesday night youth meetings. As they were welcomed and challenged to believe the Christian gospel, transformations began to occur. So improved were the lives of some of the most troubled students at Wasilla High that school administrators took note and gave Horne a reserved parking space to encourage his visits.

Over the first few years of Horne's tenure, Sarah Heath began to blossom—physically, intellectually, and spiritually. Cross-country running and the wonder-working power of an adolescent hormone surge were transforming the pudgy tomboy in glasses into a curvy, confident beauty. A vibrant, cohesive family life at home and the steadying presence of a strong, emotionally engaged father equipped Sarah with resistance to the boy craziness and premature intimacy that complicate the lives of so many young girls. She drew attention from the boys at school, of course, but her own focus was on sports and her community of faith at Wasilla Assembly.

Like most adolescents, her thoughts also began to turn to what she would do with her life. For a Christian teen, this question tends to be framed in different terms than that of a mere career choice. For as long as she could remember, Sarah had been told that God had a specific plan for every individual. This conviction transforms the typical teen floundering and flailing for purpose into one earnestly seeking the answer to a vital question: What does God want to do with my life?

It was a question that took on additional import for students under the ministry of Theron Horne. He believed that Jesus's command that his followers be *salt and light* was a mandate to transform every sphere of culture from the inside. This, in turn, meant that every vocation was *holy*, that it was a pursuit ordained by God and one in which Christians could please God no matter how mundane it might be. Horne taught his teens to reject the view that only preachers and missionaries are *called* by God. Instead, he insisted, "God has called everyone here. You might be called to be a journalist or a machinist or an oil field worker. Whatever it is, God has gifted you and planted you in that place to give Him glory. Serving God with your life doesn't necessarily mean entering full-time ministry. But we are all called. And by the way, some of you may even be called to govern. We need good people with servants' hearts in the world of politics too."[6]

Years later, Sarah would confide to Horne that these words rang a bell in her soul. Though the very idea startled the introverted teen, something about the thought of doing social good in the realm of politics stirred her as nothing else had. It was something she pondered and prayed about, even as she prepared to study journalism in college.

So profound were these lessons for Sarah Palin's life that years later, when she was about to make the speech of her life after agreeing to serve at John McCain's side, her mother made sure that credit for her daughter's rise was given where it was due. It was during the Republican Convention in Minneapolis. As it turned out, Minneapolis was where Theron Horne had landed after his years in Wasilla, and so he was much on Sally Heath's mind.

It was just hours before Sarah's big convention speech when Horne's phone rang. It was Sally Heath. After a few pleasantries, Sarah's mother got to the point: "Theron, I'm sure you know that this campaign is probably going to downplay Sarah's spiritual roots. But no matter what the books end up saying, we know who had the biggest role in launching Sarah toward this moment. We just want you to know that we recognize the impact you had. We know...and we are grateful."

Chapter 5

PROFILE: TO BE PENTECOSTAL

Great men are they who see that the spiritual is stronger than any material force.
—RALPH WALDO EMERSON

I
F MITT ROMNEY AND THE MORE THAN A DOZEN MORMONS IN the U.S. Congress are orthodox Mormons, then they believe that in the early 1800s, God the Father and Jesus Christ appeared to a teen-aged American boy and told him that all religions are in error—all Christian denominations in particular. They believe that one day, if they are good Mormons, they will become gods over their own planets, making spirit babies with spirit brides. Their commitment to large families is based in part on the belief that conceiving children on the earth provides bodies for these preexistent spirit babies in heavenly realms.

If the many Muslims spread throughout the U.S. government—including Keith Ellison, the first Muslim ever elected to Congress—are all orthodox Muslims, then they believe that Islam began in the sixth century when a spirit named Gabriel grabbed a man named Muhammad on a mountainside in Saudi Arabia and commanded the man to become his apostle. They believe that Satan takes the form of a black dog, that man was created from a clot of blood, and that one day they will drink wine from jeweled goblets on soft couches in paradise. Until then, an angel hovers over each shoulder of each Muslim, one angel recording the good deeds of the believer, the other recording the bad.

If the dozens of U.S. congressmen who are Roman Catholic, as well as the five Supreme Court justices who share their faith, are orthodox Catholics, then they believe that the wine and the bread used for Communion in a Roman Catholic mass literally change substance during the liturgy and become the body and blood of Christ. They believe that each priest is in an unbroken line of clergymen descended by ordination directly from one of the original apostles of the first century. They also believe that it is possible for the pope to speak words that the faithful are to take as the inspired truth of God.

Each of these religions is among the historic faiths of mankind. Each claims millions of followers today. Each is to be treated with respect—and each sounds far-fetched and odd to outsiders. Not too surprisingly, each is also embraced by eminent members of the U.S. government and by some of the leading politicians of our time. This is as it should be in our *e pluribus unum* nation.

Yet when Sarah Palin became the Republican vice-presidential nominee in 2008, and it became known that she had long been a member of a Pentecostal church, the grand American tradition of religious tolerance seemed to disappear. She was a heretic, bloggers claimed, and she was under the sway of modern Elmer Gantrys. Moreover, she was robotically devoted to the cult of a witch hunter. She also attended a church in which people mindlessly ranted in *tongues* and raised their hands in Nazi salutes and trained their children to be Christian versions of suicide bombers.

None of it was true, of course, but it was indicative not only of the animosity that greeted Palin from some quarters but also of the suspicion and hatred that have long been poured out on Pentecostals. Indeed, this abhorrence has become so evident in American society that it is now a mainstay of pop culture. How many times in a movie or a novel is the Pentecostal figure the murderer or the thief or the child molester? It is hard to forget the final scene in the 1991 movie *Cape Fear*, in which the Scripture-spouting murderer Max Cady, played by Robert De Niro, finally dies while shouting in tongues and spewing Bible verses as threats to characters played by Nick Nolte and Jessica Lange. Such scenes define Pentecostalism for many Americans.

Had such culture-wide suspicion of all things Pentecostal not shaped the view of Palin's faith, Americans might have learned that the movement is not what they have been led to believe. They might have learned, for example, that being Pentecostal does not automatically move one to the political right. Joshua Dubois, President Obama's head of the White House Office of Faith-Based and Neighborhood Partnerships, is a Pentecostal. He usually appears clothed and in his right mind. Americans might also have learned that Pentecostalism is no longer a movement of storefront churches and brush arbor revival meetings. Nor is it exclusively the faith of the televangelist. In fact, along with its spiritual child, the charismatic movement, Pentecostals are to be found in nearly every kind of church and denomination in the world. The lines are blurred. The movement has matured. The iconic Pentecostal is hard to find. He looks more like a passionate Baptist, an inspired Presbyterian, or perhaps an *Anglican aflame* today.

The truth is that Sarah Palin was a member of one of the fastest-growing movements in Christian history, one that must be considered mainstream today by any standard. From what could not have been but a handful of adherents when the movement began in the early 1900s, Pentecostals now number more than 580 million adherents worldwide. They are growing by more than 19 million per year, some 54,000 per day, and researchers predict that by 2025 there will be more than 1 billion Pentecostals and charismatics in the world, most located in Asia, Africa, and Latin America.[1]

It is ironic that they, and Sarah Palin, receive such approbation from the political Left. They would seem to be the religious movement of a social-justice-oriented Democrat's dream. Pentecostals are more urban than rural, more female than male, more majority world (non-Western) than Western. Their ranks are drawn from the poor (87 percent) more than the rich (13 percent). And they come from nine thousand ethno-linguistic cultures and speak more than eight thousand languages.[2] This is no uniquely Republican faith.

Pentecostals first arose from the frontier revivals and Wesleyan camp meetings of the American frontier. In the late 1800s and early 1900s, as American society became increasingly industrialized and urban, devoted Christians longed for a greater intimacy with Jesus Christ, a more genuine experience with his power, and greater success in reaching their world with the Christian gospel. Prayer meetings arose on the strength of these hopes, and, as the twentieth century dawned, revivals or *outpourings* began to occur.

One of the first took place at Bethel Bible College in Topeka, Kansas, and was led by Reverend Charles Parham. Students at the college prayed during a *watch night service* on New Year's Eve 1900 and found themselves experiencing what they later described as "the baptism of the Holy Spirit with speaking in tongues." They understood this to be what the first-century church had experienced on the Day of Pentecost when the Holy Spirit of God had filled those early believers with power and given them a prayer language that was not a known, earthly language. These Bible college students also understood that if they were indeed given what the early believers experienced, it was for the same reason: to have power to be witnesses to the world.

Word soon spread of the Topeka outpouring, and this led by 1906 to the famed Azusa Street revival from which most Pentecostals mark their birth. Guided by a legally blind, black preacher named

William Joseph Seymour, the son of former slaves from Louisiana, the meetings at Azusa Street in Los Angeles were occasions of astonishing spiritual power and personal transformation. None of the ultimate global impact of Azusa Street was betrayed by Seymour's style of ministry. As the *Los Angeles Times* quoted a witness at the time, Seymour was "meek and plain spoken and no orator. He spoke the common language of the uneducated class. He might preach for three-quarters of an hour with no more emotionalism than that there post. He was no arm-waving thunderer, by any stretch of the imagination."[3] Seymour, by all accounts a meek man of prayer, would preach from behind a stack of shoebox crates, urging the crowds not to seek spiritual experiences but rather power with which to reach the lost. His constant admonition was, "Now do not go from this meeting and talk about tongues, but try to get people saved."[4]

Perhaps because of the humility and balance that Seymour urged, the demonstrations of power at Azusa Street were dramatic. Passersby were sometimes knocked to their feet on the sidewalk. Drunks were often instantly sobered. Healings occurred, even to the satisfaction of the disbelieving press. Most importantly, lives were changed as the assembled committed themselves to Jesus Christ and to the Scriptures that Seymour preached. As a witness later said:

> No subjects or sermons were announced ahead of time, and no special speakers for such an hour. No one knew what might be coming, what God would do. All was spontaneous, ordered of the Spirit. We wanted to hear from God.... In that old building with its low rafters and bare floors, God took strong men and women to pieces and put them together again, for His glory. It was a tremendous overhauling process.[5]

The Azusa Street experience gave rise to similar meetings and outpourings throughout the world. Visitors to the tiny meetinghouse in Los Angeles, who had come from dozens of nations, returned home with stories of lives changed, with fresh interpretations of the

Bible, and with spiritual power to share. The themes of this new Christian movement became dear to millions of the faithful worldwide. There was the belief that the Holy Spirit had not left the church after the first century but was still filling the souls of the faithful, still empowering them to do miracles, still giving them knowledge from more than natural sources, and still granting them success in preaching their message to the lost.

Pentecostal meetings were passionate and emotional. Songs were sung with great energy, hands raised in honor to God. Prayers and intercession were taken seriously, for Pentecostals believed that this was more than religious ritual but rather pleading for answers from God. The Bible would be preached, and a response was expected of the congregation, often through gathering at the altar at the front of the church. There prayers would be offered for individuals, and there lives were believed to be changed by the sovereign work of the Spirit of God.

The explosive growth of the Pentecostal movement was astonishing. Its birth had come just as a world war was ravaging the earth and as technological innovation was moving many to believe that man had progressed beyond a need for God. They were helped in this by the philosophies of Freud, Darwin, and Marx. The Pentecostals answered with the message of a Jesus who filled the human soul and of a powerful Spirit from God who still changed nations and lives as he had in those great biblical tales of old.

In 1914, just as World War I was announcing itself in the *Guns of August*, a band of some 120 Pentecostals met in Hot Springs, Arkansas, to bind themselves together in a league that would become the world's largest Pentecostal denomination, the Assemblies of God. At the time, they intended only to protect the precious work of God among them and to reap greater missionary benefits as a larger body than they could as individual congregations and revival leaders. They would know their challenges, and they would make their mistakes.

There would be doctrinal disputes and church splits and the never-ceasing tension between those who clung to the old ways and those eager for the new. But they would survive, and, in time, they would blanket the world.

This was the tribe that Sarah Palin's mother, Sally, had made her own. She had been hungry for more than her Roman Catholic experience, as we have seen, and so she sought out a church that was alive and joyous and biblical and loving. She found the little Assembly of God pastored by Paul Riley, the beloved man of God who had courageously pioneered the church so many years before.

Sally and her children made this church their home and drank from its spiritual streams until each child married and moved away. It was the community they had hoped for when they first moved to Alaska. There were dinners and picnics and summer camps and people who cared when you were sick or your marriage hit bumpy seas. It was also a font of spiritual refreshing. Songs were sung so as to lift the soul to God, and sermons were preached as though they were the final word of God to be spoken on the earth. Always there were the calls to the altar for prayer after the sermon, to make the words spoken a reality in the heart. Sally would be there often, as would each of her children from time to time.

It was a defining experience for the future governor of Alaska. She would know people both wealthier and poorer than her family and love them just the same. Through the prayers and compassionate sharing of a loving community, she would hear of the hardship and the darkness of the world—of the man who beat his wife and the couple whose marriage wasn't going to survive and the children who were caught stealing from a local store. There were groups who visited prisoners and groups who cared for newcomers to the community and groups who made sure the destitute weren't alone. She saw the hard drinking changed and made into pillars of character, and she saw the grieving comforted and empowered to move on. This was what it meant to be in a church like Wasilla Assembly of God.

Did she sit next to people who spoke in tongues? Certainly. Did she hear people offer aloud what they thought were prophecies? Undoubtedly. Did she see attempts to cast out demons, and did she pray with her fellow believers for some miracle in their town? Yes.

She was also told that she had a destiny, that there was some role of service for which she had been made. It might be as a doctor or as a teacher or as a missionary or as a politician, but she was made for a purpose, and that purpose was about doing good for others. This was the message her church labored to embed in her heart: that there were works prepared for her to do before she was even born, and that she should be careful how she lived since she had been entrusted with the grace of God.

By the time she was running for the vice presidency in 2008, all of this sweetness and nobility was shoved aside by the press. In an incredibly unwise move, the new pastor of Wasilla Assembly of God chose to put videos of Sarah Palin speaking at the church or Sarah Palin receiving prayer on YouTube. It took the inner life of the church and put it on display to an uninitiated world, and it left Sarah Palin looking like the pawn of preachers and religious extremes.

It grew worse. There was an African pastor, named Bishop Muthee, who often visited Wasilla Assembly. He was a valiant man of faith and compassion, but he had been depicted in a film called *Transformations* leading a move to pray a witch out of an African village. The film had made the rounds in American churches and had made Muthee something of a hero to some American evangelicals. Yet, as seriously as Africans take the subject of witches, American journalists find it a misguided belief from a misguided time. Muthee became *the witch hunter*, and Palin his deceived disciple. The film of his prayer for her, which included him praying in tongues, made the rounds on the Internet and was used to embarrass the Republican campaign and discredit the Pentecostal community.

The press did not report the fact that the unwise pastor at Wasilla Assembly of God was urged by his superiors to remove the film clips from the church's Web site, did so, and apologized. Unreported went the truth that not all Pentecostals speak in tongues. Unreported went the good done by Wasilla Assembly in its community and by churches like it in communities the world over. And unreported went the ennobling impact of Wasilla Assembly on Sarah Palin and the reality that much of what she had achieved had been due to the faith, character, vision, and discipline that had been pressed into her life by that same Pentecostal church.

But there is a larger issue than one campaign. The presence of Sarah Palin on our national stage presses the question of Pentecostalism's acceptance in American society, and this is a question whose answer is long overdue. Pentecostalism is, after all, the preferred religious expression of a quarter of the world's two billion Christians, and it is also the most successful social movement of the past century.[6] Moreover, there is nothing Pentecostals believe that is any stranger than the beliefs of Mormons, Muslims, or Roman Catholics, many of whom populate American government on both sides of the political divide.

Perhaps Pentecostalism's day has come. Perhaps it is time to end the attacks on this widely held faith, much as our culture has insisted on ending bigoted portrayals of blacks and one-dimensional portrayals of women. And when that day of acceptance comes, Sarah Palin, perhaps along with such unlikely fellows as former Attorney General John Ashcroft and Obama administration official Joshua Dubois, may be seen as a pioneer of Pentecostalism in American public life—and no longer numbered among the deceived and the extreme.

Chapter 6

TODD

Do what thy manhood bids thee do,
from none but self expect applause;
He noblest lives and noblest dies
who makes and keeps his self-made laws.[1]
—SIR RICHARD FRANCIS BURTON

I<small>T IS</small> S<small>EPTEMBER</small> 5, 2008. T<small>HE</small> R<small>EPUBLICAN</small> C<small>ONVENTION IN</small> Minneapolis, Minnesota, has just come to an end. It has been a week since John McCain announced Sarah Palin as his vice-presidential nominee, two days since Palin gave the speech of her life, and not even twenty-four hours since McCain accepted his party's nomination for president of the United States.

Now, it is all over. And just about to begin. The McCain campaign, riding high on the bounce in the polls it received from the Palin appointment, has roared out of the convention on a tour of key cities. John and Cindy McCain are taking Palin on the national tour they hope will turn this election in their favor. The Great Game is now underway. The Straight Talk Express is on the move.

But Todd Palin, Sarah's husband, is not on board.

Instead, he has remained behind in Minneapolis. It turns out that Hay Days, one of the largest snowmobile conventions in the country and the symbolic beginning of snowmobile season, is being held near Minneapolis. Todd Palin intends to be there.

And so he was. While his wife campaigned for the vice presidency of the United States, Todd Palin attended Hay Days. He signed autographs—as a four-time winner of the Iron Dog snowmobile race in Alaska, he is something of a rock star at this convention—and he watched snowmobiles race on grass. He drank beer, he talked insider gossip with snowmobile company reps, and he toured the exhibits. Then, only when Hay Days was over, and only when Todd was ready, did he rejoin his wife on the campaign trail.

This was in keeping with the manner of the man. For Todd Palin, politics is not primary. Life is primary. He is proud of his governor wife and supports her nearly as well as any man can, but Todd is his own man. For him, life is about the work of a man's hands and the machines he masters and the rowdy ways of a band of brothers and the love he has for his family and for the land. It is about flying your own plane around the Talkeetna Mountains or snowmobiling with your daughter or having a beer and a laugh with some friends while standing around a dismantled engine. Life is not posturing, something you fabricate for public view. Life is what you make as you apply who you are to the challenges of this world with those you hold dear.

It is pleasant to think of how much good might have been done for the country had Todd Palin taken up residence in Washington DC with his wife, the vice president. Politics and government aside, it might have been wonderful to behold. There, in the city of the androgynous politician, where image and word pass for character and deed, it might have helped change something in the national psyche for a man who spoke little, did much, and lived simply to go about his quiet, manly ways. It might have reminded us of what the words *common man* once meant, of what it looks like for the calm nobility of American virtues to pull on its jeans and go about its business each day.

It might have confused many Americans, though, for Todd Palin is the embodiment of the seeming contradictions that true manhood always is. He is the kind of fierce competitor who can take on the nearly two thousand miles of the Iron Dog snowmobile race in Alaska, get thrown seventy feet when his machine hits a snow-covered barrel, break his arm, and still finish fourth in the race. But he can also stand quietly in the back of a room holding a sleeping baby while his wife makes a speech, content to stay out of view while his politician spouse claims the limelight.

He is also the kind of man who can lovingly welcome his daughter's boyfriend into his home and into his life, but then when that boyfriend betrays his trust, make a menacing impression on the young man's mind. "Todd walked in looking like he was going to rip my head off," remembered Levi Johnston of the moment when he told Todd and Sarah Palin he had gotten their daughter pregnant. "I was ready for an ass whooping."[2] Most men in America who heard understood—and admired.

Todd Palin is the kind of man who can have a door-slamming, yelling argument with his wife, but then clean the house and feed the children while that same wife leaves home to attend yet another political event. He's the kind of man who says little and speaks of his faith even less, but who, upon seeing his wife's torment over the news that the child she is carrying has Down's syndrome, turns to her and says, "It's going to be OK." And when that wife, in an uncharacteristic moment of self-pity, cries out, "Why us?" that husband replies, "Why not us?" and then in an eager, fatherly way begins pondering what life with his new son will be like: "What will he want to do?...Will he want to tinker with me in the garage? Will he want to ride on the four-wheeler and drive the skiff? I'm going to build him a buoy swing. I bet he'll love to fly with me."[3] And in the joy of fatherhood, the subject of his son's special need is rarely mentioned again.

There is a theory that the more distant men are from nature—the less they work with their hands and harvest the earth and the sea and live lives gently conditioned by the cycles of creation—the less centered and balanced and, well, normal they are. If this is true, then it may be Todd Palin's greatest secret. He lives a joyously satisfied life largely because he revels in labor and land and in the muscular pursuits that have defined his days. The names of his children tell the tale. The Palins' oldest son, Track, was so named because he was born during track and field season. Their oldest daughter, Bristol, was named for the bay where Todd has fished all his life. Willow, their second daughter, was named for the Alaskan state bird, the willow ptarmigan. And their youngest daughter, Piper, was named for Todd's airplane, a Piper Cub. Even the Palins' youngest child, Trig, has a name associated with Todd's love of the physical life and the natural world. He is named for Todd's great uncle, a Bristol Bay fisherman, who fished those many seasons with Todd and taught him much of what he knew about the ways of the sea and the life of a fisherman. Todd wanted to honor both the memories of fishing seasons past and the memory of the man in the naming of his son.

Indeed, fishing and family defined much of Todd Palin's early life. He was born on September 6, 1964, in a small fishing village called Dillingham, which was so remote it was accessible only by boat or plane. He grew up learning the ways of the *set net* fisherman. In set netting, fishermen string long nets between underwater posts. Fish become entangled in these nets, are gathered up by workers on twenty-seven-foot boats with outboard engines, and are taken to the various canneries by yet other boats designed for the task. When the salmon run each June and July, the harvest can be as great as two hundred pounds an hour. There is hardly time to eat or sleep, but the potential for huge profit is great.

Todd would learn well the ways of his family's fishing business, but he would also give himself to his love of nearly all outdoor pursuits. He hunted; he drove snowmobiles; he explored deep into the interior of Alaska. Always there was his life on the sea. He was also a gifted athlete, particularly on the basketball court. When his parents' divorce eventually meant a move to Wasilla to live with his father, it was his basketball ability that first gained him fame in the small Matanuska-Susitna Valley town.

Another basketball player, young Sarah Heath, was impressed with Todd's skills on the court, and also by his industry. While still in high school, Todd owned his own car and his own truck, was part owner of a business, and had several snowmobiles to his name. Sarah had never known anyone like him. He was confident. He was earthy. He was prosperous for his age and background. It is revealing of the Heath family culture that Sarah's parents were drawn to Todd because he was both hardworking and polite—and because he loved Alaska as much as they did.

This last trait was no light matter to the Heaths. Todd is part Yupik Eskimo, and this was both a genetic and a cultural force in his life. He had learned from childhood a mystical form of love for and attachment to the land. The land spoke to him, empowered him. He drew from it, felt it as an inner force as well as an outer reality. It was something he would eventually come to share with Chuck Heath, Sarah's father. Indeed, the two men are much alike, and it is not hard to envision them standing side by side before one of Alaska's magnificent vistas in complete silence, both men honoring a meaningful moment in the Yupik way—with a noble quiet befitting the holiness of the scene.

It was not only Todd's love of Alaska that endeared him to the Heaths, but also his infectious love of work. He had determined early in his life that he would distinguish himself by simply working harder than other men. It gained him admiration as well as prosperity. He would toil harder than men twice his age, love it twice as much, and gain the confidence of those who employed him. He would rise and always be looked upon as a man who could be trusted. Because he was happy, he was pleasant to be with, and this too made him a valued worker. All of these traits were evident to the Heaths as they watched Todd stack their firewood or clean an animal carcass or serve the family in his competent, good-natured way. They came to love him and were eager to welcome him into their lives.

First, though, came the college years, and for Todd these seemed not to be as much the season of maturing and emerging that they were for Sarah. She would attend the University of Hawaii, then return home to attend local colleges before finally graduating from the University of Idaho. Her vision sharpened, her skills increased, and her confidence solidified. Todd started at the same local colleges as Sarah, but they didn't seem a fit. He played basketball, which was his true passion, and eventually ended up at Missouri Valley College in Marshall, Missouri. He was an all-heart player who impressed his coaches, but the other players were bigger and better than those he had known, and he could not seriously compete. Besides, this was his first experience apart from the land that was his life, and he felt himself shriveling inside when he was *outside*. He returned to Wasilla and Dillingham, never finished his degree, and began hoping for a job with British Petroleum on Alaska's oil-rich North Slope.

He seems to have lost a sense of himself during this time. Perhaps with Sarah away and with no work to define him, he began to lose his grip on who he was. In 1986, after an evening of drinking with buddies, he made the mistake of driving himself home. He was pulled over by police, ticketed for driving under the influence of alcohol, and taken to jail. It would remain on his record permanently and seemed to lend credence to the picture some later attempted to paint of Todd as a typical, hard-drinking, irresponsible Eskimo. It wasn't true, but the shame of it fueled his determination to live the slur down.

This raises the matter of his faith. When Sarah had first fallen for Todd, she had been concerned that he was not a Christian as she was. Todd cussed. He chewed tobacco. He did not go to church. He was a good and gentle soul with a mystical view of life, but this alone did not satisfy Sarah's evangelical standards. Then Todd told her that he had committed his life to Jesus Christ at a sports camp some years before. It satisfied her, though she realized that Todd, like her father, found God more in the cathedral of nature than in any steepled building, and it would likely always be that way. Choosing character and reverence over church attendance and religious conformity, Sarah decided she could be one with Todd in all things, including spiritual matters.

It is revealing of the life of the set-net fisherman that Todd and Sarah eloped in August of 1988, largely because the fishing season that year had not produced a good yield. There was no bitterness or anger. This was simply life, submitted as it was in all things to the demands of nature. Todd and Sarah would begin their lives sharing a small apartment with Sarah's sisters, while Todd did odd jobs and awaited word of work with British Petroleum. Finally it came, and Todd and Sarah began living out the rhythms of the Alaska oilman, with the weeks away from home and the strains a young couple almost always have with time, budgets, absences, and dreams.

Sarah was likely the greater dreamer of the two, and Todd likely realized early on that his wife nursed a sense of destiny that he did not share. She had been taught at her Assembly of God church that she had a calling, a purpose determined by God. This would be somehow involved in serving others, but it was a calling just the same, as certain as the calling any preacher ever knew. Todd saw this emerge progressively in Sarah—as she decided to serve on her school district's PTA, and later as she ran for Wasilla's mayor, and then, surely surprising to him, for Alaska's governor. He would joke publicly later that he wished he had paid more attention when Sarah said she was getting involved in the PTA, but this was only a joke. He had been there, all along, standing with her as she fulfilled that burning sense of purpose that she understood was a gift from God.

What Todd could best offer Sarah was the gift of his quiet, confident, protective manhood. He was Yupik, after all—more poignant in silence than a white man was with words. So as he simply stood wordlessly with his wife, and while she fulfilled her public roles, he spoke to her of his love and his belief in a voice she had learned to hear. He had come from a cultural tradition that recognized female leadership, in which men had learned to respect the gifts of women without feeling diminished or dismissed. Todd understood that this was his role. It would not always be easy, and he would sometimes be attacked by critics when he did give his wife advice on matters he knew well—petroleum or conservation or care for Alaska's natives. But he was made of sterner stuff and did not crumble as some political spouses might. This became obvious during the vice-presidential campaign when he was photographed wearing a T-shirt that sported the words: "If you don't love America, why don't you get the hell out?" He knew it would create a stir. He knew it would draw fire. But in true Yupik way, he said what he had to say, and he did not intend to explain. Point made.

In return for all that Todd offered Sarah, she celebrated the rare brand of masculinity that was his gift to her. When Todd was thrown seventy feet from his snowmobile while on that Iron Dog race, Sarah did not seem to flinch. "These are big boys," she exulted. "They make their own decisions. They're hard-core Alaskans doing hard-core adventures. I totally support him, and I totally support the race. I love it."

And then, with a flirty, bashful glance toward Todd, she said, "Going four hundred miles with a broken arm, that's impressive!"

And so it was.

Section 1 Afterword

FOUR TRUTHS FROM SARAH PALIN'S BEGINNINGS

1. Family has fashioned her soul.

Nobel Prize–winning historian David McCullough delights in telling of how his children often say he will never be a great writer because he is not tortured enough. He tells this, of course, to wring a laugh, but there is truth in it. Pain, hardship, and wounding are often the price that the artistic soul, the lofty visionary, and the fiery orator pay for greatness. There is something about early suffering that opens the heart, grants it sensitivities it would not otherwise have, and allows it to perceive in ways the comfortable will never know. A columnist watching the presidential debate between Al Gore and George W. Bush later wrote, "You wish that they had both suffered more." It was a hope for gravitas, for a depth of compassion and vision that the columnist thought both men, through their relatively easy early lives, lacked.

Palin might be viewed in much the same way. She does not have the tortured tale; she is not Lincoln pushing back against the darkness or Churchill almost literally haunted by his father or even Barack Obama with his fatherless search for belonging. Palin is just what she appears to be—centered, whole, and happy. Indeed, the phrase *happy warrior* was seldom used of anyone more aptly.

This is unquestionably a result of her family's influence upon her. She had a strong, loving father; a mother of generosity and depth; and brothers and sisters raised on discipline, work, and the joy of the grand adventure. Her upbringing, the uniqueness of living in Alaska aside, was nearly ideal, healthy, and rich. It has left an imprint upon her.

She is unique among those who populate our public life because she is not angry, raging, bombastic, or rude. She does not approach politics from a wounded, vindictive state. Instead, she is about her ideas and her vision because all else is in order in her life. This makes her energetic, even perky, which thrills her supporters but can irritate her foes.

What she may lack is introspection, the gift for soul searching that the lonely, the bruised, and the wronged naturally have. It may cause her answers to come too easily, her principles to be too unexamined. It can make her come off as a lightweight. She is not, of course, but this is the downside of the healthy, happy childhood she enjoyed, and she should know it and seek to dig a deeper well.

2. Alaska and the idea of the state are primary for Palin.

For most Americans, the state in which they live is a source of occasional pride and celebration, but it does not shape the way they see the world. They wear the colors of the state school during football season or claim bragging rights at parties, but their state is simply a place to live and to celebrate from time to time.

For Sarah Palin, Alaska is a world apart by which she understands all else. Her family did not happen to live in Alaska; they chose it for its ruggedness and its mystique. They lived there by whatever means they could because it spoke to them and gave their lives a meaning they found in no other place. They loved their state, absorbed its meaning, and put it at the core of their lives.

Palin came to understand that Alaska is such a unique place that outsiders could seldom understand, particularly outsiders in Washington DC or in corporate offices in other cities of the world. Alaskans would have to guard their treasures and make sure that their destiny was as much as possible in their own hands. This belief defined Palin's leadership in the state, and it defines her political philosophy as well.

Her experience in Alaska led her to believe in the uniqueness and the integrity of each state. She advocates a resurgent federalism, one in which the needs of states are addressed by the creativity of the people at the most local level rather than by a uniformity imposed from outside. For example, she applauds Arizona's controversial immigration laws because she believes that each state ought to have the authority to address its own pressing needs.[1] She has cheered Louisiana governor Bobby Jindal in developing rapid solutions to the BP oil disaster rather than waiting for a glacial federal response.[2] This is the genius of the federal system, she believes: that the uniqueness and ingenuity of the American people prevail at the most local level to solve problems and advance freedom. Alaska has taught her this, and it is a central pillar of her politics.

3. Palin has been influenced by the Eskimo view of women.

When Hillary Clinton conceded her presidential campaign to Barack Obama, she used a beautiful metaphor for the ascent of women: "Although we weren't able to shatter that highest, hardest glass ceiling this time, thanks to you, it's got about 18 million cracks in it....And the light is shining through like never before, filling us all with the hope and the sure knowledge that the path will be a little easier next time."[3] It was a stirring statement that captured how many women feel about acquiring power in American society.

As moving as it was, it is unlikely that Sarah Palin would express herself that way. She is proud to be a woman who has accomplished much, but she does not feel the struggle or the battle for rights as other women do. The fact is that she grew up in a culture that already honored women in leadership, and this has shaped how she sees herself and what she believes about the rise of women.

Not only was Palin raised in a Pentecostal culture in which women are seen as uniquely gifted by God, but she also absorbed the Eskimo culture around her and its belief that women have special powers to offer the rest of the tribe. The tradition of the wise woman, the supernaturally empowered female, runs deep in Eskimo culture. In fact, in Inuit belief, the closest thing to a deity is the *Old Woman* (*Sedna*) who is believed to live beneath the sea.[4] In Eskimo culture, men defer to women on many matters, and in traditional councils never is a weighty matter decided without hearing from the wise women in their midst.

Palin not only absorbed this from the nearby Eskimo culture, but she also had it reinforced in her life once she married Todd. He is a Yupik Eskimo himself and was accustomed to the gifted woman wielding authority and being honored by the tribe. He has taken the backseat to her political rise without rancor, for this is simply the way of nature as he and his tribe understand it.

Palin herself will celebrate the power of being a woman, but she will not become a primary champion of women's issues. For her, women in leadership and authority are a natural condition of life, one that arises best when freedom and prosperity prevail.

4. Palin lives and leads from a sense of divine destiny.

From the earliest days of her life, Sarah Palin was taught that she had a destiny. This sprang naturally from the scriptures that she read, from the teaching she heard in church, and from the counsel of her mother in a thousand matters. As Palin tells it, destiny was even urged on the basketball court. In *Going Rogue*, she recounts that when her basketball coach didn't celebrate some achievement of hers as she thought he should, he would retort, "You were put there to do this, so don't act surprised."

"I believe—and still do," she has written, "that each person has a destiny, a reason for being."[5] This belief has marked her. It has made her look for opportunities to advance that she might otherwise have missed. It has made her bold in defense of her principles since she believes she has been positioned to expound them by the hand of

God. It also has enabled her to endure torturous seasons with grace, since she believes that these too are part of God's plan.

Those who do not believe in a divine plan, in providence super-intending all things, will expect that such a view would make one arrogant, self-important, and vain. But the biblical concept of destiny should produce humility and concern for others. In fact, the whole idea of a divine destiny in Christianity is that one is positioned to serve, to tend the needs of others to the glory of God. This is what Palin believes and strives to live, and it will be a hallmark of her politics all her days.

Section 2

POLITICS

Chapter 7

INTO THE FRAY

*Politics is war without bloodshed while war is politics with
bloodshed.*[1]

—MAO TSE-TUNG
"ON PROTRACTED WAR"

THE YEAR 1992 WAS A TURNING POINT IN THE LIFE OF SARAH
Palin. It was the year she began to step into the calling she
had first envisioned for herself during her days in the youth ministry
of Wasilla Assembly of God. Had she not departed from her routine,
had she not dreamt of something more, she might never have entered
the pages of American history. It is likely that duty, labor, and the
tyranny of the immediate would have prevailed, for Sarah Palin was
nothing if not a woman of devotion to work.

Work had been a hallmark of her life. In addition to the rigors that
came with growing up in the Heath family, she had earned her own
spending money since the age of twelve and had paid her own way
through college. She had done this through a variety of demanding
jobs, including as a hand on Todd's salmon fishing boat, waiting
tables, gutting fish, or processing crab at various canneries—a hard,
smelly type of drudgery Alaskans call "working on a slime line." Her
only departure from tough physical labor was her now-famous stint

in the world of beauty pageants. By winning Miss Wasilla in 1981 and being Miss Congeniality at the Miss Alaska pageant, Sarah earned enough in scholarship money to pay for a year of school. It was one of the few times in her early life that money had come with relative ease.

Upon graduation from college, Sarah had begun working as a sports reporter at two Anchorage television stations. Eager to rise in her profession, she took a break from this role only to have her first baby, Track, and then immediately returned to work. She had dreams and thought that television might fulfill them. Then, things changed. She suffered a heartbreaking miscarriage not long after Track was born. Soon pregnant again, she prayed long hours for a healthy baby. When Bristol arrived, a happy gurgling gift, Sarah began to reassess her college dreams of becoming a nationally known network sports reporter. She loved being a mom and was finding fulfillment and excitement in that role. Besides, advancing in television sports would have required frequent moves to ever larger media markets. The thought of leaving the valley she loved grew less appealing with each passing year. She eventually cut her work in television to just weekends and the occasional fill-in role for a vacationing sports anchor.

This shift was possible, in part, because money had become less of an issue for the Palins. Todd had gotten that long-awaited job on the North Slope oilfields, though the move involved a tradeoff for the young couple. Todd would be bringing home much more money, but doing so meant that he was gone for a week or more at a time. Almost everyone in Alaska had seen this arrangement take a toll on marriages. The divorce rate among North Slope workers was appallingly high. In 1990, Alaska's overall divorce rate of 5.5 divorces per thousand married couples was the twelfth highest in the nation.[2] But some studies indicated that for couples with one spouse away on the slope half of the time, the marriage casualty rate was more than double that figure.

Todd and Sarah's relationship seemed to be made of sterner stuff. It had remained strong throughout their college years, though they rarely saw each other. There was no reason to believe it would not survive an oilman's life. Much of the credit for this was due to Sarah's extensive network of support in Wasilla. It included her mother and sisters, many close relationships at Wasilla Assembly of God, and a community of friends built during more than two decades in the Mat-Su Valley. All of these made a difference and lessened the loneliness of Todd's many absences.

At the center of Sarah's social life was a tight-knit group of five women who sarcastically called themselves the *Elite Six*. This sextet met and bonded at the aerobics studio two of them owned. The Jane Fonda–led aerobics craze that swept America in the late 1980s had even reached remote Wasilla. Fitness-minded Sarah, eager to lose her baby weight and able to run outdoors only in the late spring and summer, embraced aerobics with Chuck Heath–like abandon. So in love was she with this new movement that she once showed up at an Elite Six costume party dressed as Fonda, the reigning American fitness queen. Sarah cut a hilarious figure since she was many months pregnant at the time.

Another key circle in Sarah's life was a small group of women from church who gathered regularly to pray. They helped each other hold the usual concerns before their God—children, husbands, and family finances, for example. Sometimes the needs were more desperate. At one point, Sarah quietly called upon the group to pray intently for her. Doctors had discovered a lesion in her breast. Soon after, a biopsy was performed. Each prayer group member interceded with urgency for Sarah, and tension filled the days afterward as all waited for the results. When the call finally came, it brought good news: *benign*.[3]

Relief and joy filled the Palin home at news of the good lab results, but soon there seemed to be a subtle change in Sarah. She had endured a *cancer scare*, and it had made her contemplate the meaning of her life. She was certainly happy with her life. There were the love of Todd and the delight she felt at her amazing children. Still, if life was indeed so tenuous, so easily changed, perhaps she ought to be about the higher business of her existence. Perhaps she ought to move more intentionally in the direction she sensed for her future.

As a young girl, the thought that God may have destined her for the realm of politics stirred her. Now, in the wake of this health scare and with time aside to ponder her journey, Sarah thought she felt the return of that old sense of calling, the draw toward making a difference and on a more public stage.

Wasilla was changing. Growing. And not always gracefully.

When the Heaths moved to the Mat-Su Valley in 1969, the official population was only about three hundred people. A drive into Anchorage took an hour and a half even in good weather. The town wasn't even officially incorporated until 1974, and by the 1990s it still didn't have basic services such a police force. Law enforcement and crime investigation were still handled by a smattering of state troopers—when they had time.

In 1971, the George Parks Highway was built through the swampy marsh flats at the mouth of the Matanuska River, cutting the trip to Anchorage in half. Suddenly, living in Wasilla became a viable, much more affordable option for people with jobs in Anchorage. It was also an ideal home base for families with a member working on the North Slope—families like the Palins. Wasilla's population surged and diversified. New businesses sprang up along the highways. By 1990, Wasilla was home to more than four thousand people, and the wider Matanuska-Susitna Borough had swelled to more than forty thousand.

In the minds of some, all of this growth created the need for new local government services and regulations. And where there is government, politics invariably follow.

In early 1992, twenty-eight-year-old Sarah rendezvoused at the local fitness club with her Elite Six buddies for an aerobics class three days a week at 6:00 a.m. They weren't alone. Among the other early-morning regulars were Wasilla mayor John Stein and his wife and a retired Anchorage police captain named Irl Stambaugh. Another faithful aerobicizer was the fifty-one-year-old father of one of Sarah's high school classmates, Nick Carney. He was also the uncle of Michelle Carney, the other unhappy player sent down to play on the junior varsity team along with Sarah when the girls were both juniors in high school.

Though Nick Carney's roots were deep in Wasilla, he was a classic example of what locals called a *Brooks Brothers* Alaskan. This was a term some pioneer Alaskans invented—with only mild scorn—for an Alaskan who had acquired his education outside the state only to return with novel ideas for change. Carney's parents had moved to Wasilla in the mid-1950s and homesteaded there when he was fifteen years old. Three years later, he graduated as the valedictorian in a Wasilla senior class of five. He occasionally joked about having graduated in the top 20 percent of his class. "In fact, I *was* the top 20 percent of my class," he would add.

Jokes aside, his academic abilities were real. He was accepted to Dartmouth College in New Hampshire. Four years later, with an Ivy League degree in his hands, he moved to Juneau and worked in the private sector for five years before accepting a job with the state. This new assignment took him to Anchorage to run the state office of economic development. When the new, shortcut highway was complete, he moved back to Wasilla and commuted to Anchorage, even after being named head of the state's agriculture department.

After an early retirement, Carney launched a Wasilla-based garbage hauling business. Prior to this, all Wasilla residents had no choice but to periodically load up their garbage and haul it to the local dump. Afterward, they could pay Carney's company to haul their garbage for them, and this ingenuity was typical of Carney's custom blend of entrepreneurship and devotion to civic improvement.

Carney was a key member of a group of local business owners working on ways to guide Wasilla through its growing pains and improve the business climate. The group—officially named *Watch on Wasilla*—viewed the city's lack of a police force as one of the primary obstacles to attracting more businesses. Admittedly, crime was rare, but burglaries and shoplifting in the area were rising in concert with the population. The widely scattered state troopers simply did not have a high enough profile to deter such crimes, nor did they have the resources to investigate them when they occurred.

Money was the principal barrier to establishing a Wasilla police force. The city had a property tax levy that helped pay for the local schools and some infrastructure, but there was no sales tax. Watch on Wasilla wanted the city council to approve a 2 percent sales tax on purchases within the city, with a cap of ten dollars tax on purchases larger than five hundred dollars. They found little support for the idea on the city council, the majority of whom were from the old Wasilla pioneer families. People are rarely interested in increasing taxes on themselves, and a majority on the current council was clearly of the *if-it-ain't-broke-don't-fix-it* philosophy.

Carney and company decided the only solution was to change the balance of power on the council by filling a couple of the seats with more forward-thinking individuals. For the 1992 elections, Carney decided to run in his ward, but the group still needed a candidate for the race in a neighboring ward. The group knew they ideally needed someone young, energetic, and appealing to the mothers of school-age children—those who comprised the fastest-growing demographic group in the city.

After some discussion, the name of Sarah Palin rose as a consensus favorite. Not only did she fit the bill in terms of profile, but Sarah also brought the added benefit of being fully acceptable to both sides of the cultural divide in Wasilla. As the daughter of Chuck and Sally Heath and the wife of Todd Palin, she had instant credibility with the pioneers. For the more recent arrivals fleeing the high cost of real estate in Anchorage, Sarah had been a familiar face on their television sets in her work reporting sports news. In the eyes of people like Carney, though Sarah had gone to a series of nondescript colleges, she at least had left Alaska for her education. That didn't exactly make her a fellow Brooks Brothers Alaskan, but for these leading progressive lights in Wasilla it was good enough.

In other words, she brought the ability to speak to both the rednecks and the Brooks Brothers Alaskans, the pioneers and the hockey moms, the Cheechakos and the Sourdoughs. It was a rare and powerful advantage.

Carney approached Sarah about the race, and after some prayer and discussion, she agreed to run. Much of the motivation for the decision came from the words of Theron Horne: "Some are called to realms of politics." For the first time in her life, the words that had resonated in her soul all these years could now begin to be fulfilled.

Friends later reported that it was as though Sarah was fired from a cannon. Carney offered some elementary instruction in door-to-door campaigning, and Sarah was off to win the world. While Todd worked on the North Slope, she loaded Track and Bristol in a Red Flyer wagon and pulled them through neighborhoods knocking on doors and dropping off campaign brochures featuring the headline slogan "Positive-ly Palin." Sarah's entire network pitched in—her family, the Elite Six, and even members of her church. It was the kind of local race in which Republican and Democrat labels mean nothing. Victory is about positions on issues only slightly more than it is about reputation and who your people are.

For all these reasons, Sarah won. It speaks loudly of the unusual nature of the area's political sensibilities that in the presidential election decided on that same day, the Matanuska-Susitna Borough was carried, not by the moderate Republican George H. W. Bush, nor by the victorious Arkansas Democrat Bill Clinton. Instead, it was one of only a handful of counties in America won by a maverick Texas billionaire espousing traditional moral and economic values—third-party candidate Ross Perot. Apparently, mavericks appealed to the people of the Mat-Su Valley.

Nick Carney won his race as well, and Sarah eagerly went to work with him to pass the 2 percent sales tax as well as the measure establishing Wasilla's first police department. Indeed, a few months later, she looked on as her fellow aerobicizer, Irl Stambaugh, was sworn in as the city's first police chief, overseeing a freshly hired force of eight full-time officers.

Palin gave herself to her new role. In her autobiography she relates a humorous story of having a two-hour telephone conversation with a constituent about sewage treatment one evening while her exasperated husband gave her *wind it up* hand signals from across the living room. The fact is, she became a hungry, driven student of everything involving city government—sewage, garbage, fire fighting, insurance liability, state subsidies, as well as state regulations and mandates. And she was a quick study.

So quick in fact, that midway through the second year of her three-year term, Palin grew sufficiently confident in her understanding of city processes and in her convictions about the issues facing Wasilla that she began butting heads with Carney and his close ally, Mayor John Stein, on a variety of issues. This initially had to come as a surprise to Carney, who thought he had in Palin not only an ally but also a protégée. He reasonably assumed she understood that the most-prized commodity in political life is loyalty. But here and throughout her political rise, Sarah demonstrated that her overriding loyalty was to her principles. Time and again she would disappoint a former mentor, alienate a potential ally, or send a friend away empty-handed if her internal moral compass pointed a different direction.

It was in that second year on the city council that Sarah and Todd welcomed their third child to the family. Willow was born on July 5, 1994, with Todd away at the summer fishing grounds on Bristol Bay. Sarah was kayaking with friends on a lake just north of Wasilla when she went into labor, an almost irresponsible act typical of her own personal answer to the call of the wild. Pregnancy kept Sarah from nothing she wanted to enjoy of the Alaskan outdoors.

While the joy of a new baby girl brightened and busied everything at home, Sarah's work on the city council grew increasingly challenging. The source of the growing friction between Sarah, Nick Carney, and Mayor Stein is still a matter of some dispute. Palin has described her time on the council as an ongoing confrontation with a "good old boys" network and as a liberal-versus-conservative clash over policy. In her autobiography she makes much of a stand she took in opposition to a certain proposed ordinance backed by Mayor Stein and his faction, Nick Carney included. The law required Wasilla's citizens to utilize a garbage collection service rather than leaving them free to haul their trash to the dump themselves. It is easy to understand how those who wanted to beautify Wasilla and improve the city's image wanted to stop the ubiquitous sight of pickup trucks filled with loose garbage heading out to the landfill. It is equally easy to imagine that those who shared Palin's libertarian reflexes might think the city ought to mind its own darned business.

In *Going Rogue*, Palin depicts her opposition to the law as a principled stand against corruption and argues that Carney "spearheaded" the charge for the ordinance even though he owned the city's only garbage hauling service and would therefore personally profit from the sharp increase in business that would result. That is not the recollection of Stein and Carney.

There is reliable truth in the old cliché about every story having two sides. Carney's take on this episode got a full airing in a long article in the October 2008 issue of left-of-center magazine *The New Republic*. In a piece by Noam Scheiber titled "Barracuda: The Resentments of Sarah Palin," Carney and another member of the council at that time recall that Carney recused himself from the garbage ordinance because of the conflict of interest.[4]

It certainly seems reasonable that a person with Carney's extensive experience in state government would be aware of such a glaring ethical conflict and take pains to avoid the appearance of impropriety. Carney does state, however, that some council members brought him into discussions of the ordinance as a sort of expert witness on the logistics of garbage hauling. It is not difficult to imagine Palin viewing Carney's participation as a prearranged backroom play.

The *New Republic* article presents Palin's opposition to this specific proposal and her conflicts with Carney in general as a manifestation of her antielitist resentments and insecurities. It seems more likely, however, that these battles are simply a product of a much older, more universal war—the age-old contest between those with confidence in the power of central planning to improve society and those who believe central planning restricts liberty, ultimately fails to deliver, and produces negative unintended consequences. Put more simply, this is the battle between those with progressive ideals and those with libertarian principles.

Palin is clearly a libertarian in these matters, and her libertarian instincts are reinforced by a thick-skinned tenacity. These, combined with her innate tendencies to question authority systems, react strongly to perceived injustice, and reject elitist posturing, are not a formula for political compromise. This surely contributed to the crises on the Wasilla city council.

Still, she was obviously championing the views of many of her constituents since she was reelected by a wide margin to a second three-year term. Her confidence was growing, her understanding of the issues deepening, her political skills sharpening. Before long, she began to realize that she yearned for greater authority, a greater power to do good, and she began to contemplate a run for mayor. It was a decision that defined all that would follow in her life. Had she tired of politics and returned to private life, she might never have become known outside of her small town. Yet she carried within her a sense of destiny that would not rest. She also had a strength of personality and conviction that drew her to power, that allowed her to see what could be done if her skills and worldview were wedded with political possibilities. After taking counsel with her husband, her family, and her friends, she determined that becoming Wasilla's mayor was her destined next step.

Chapter 8

REALIGNMENT: THE CULTURE WAR COMES TO THE VALLEY

There is a flow to history and culture. This flow is rooted and has its wellspring in the thoughts of people.... The results of their thought-world flow through their fingers or from their tongues into the external world. This is true of Michelangelo's chisel, and it is true of a dictator's sword.[1]
—FRANCIS SCHAEFFER
How Should We Then Live?

SARAH PALIN HAD WON. IT WAS NEWS THAT ROLLED THROUGH the Mat-Su Valley, shocking nearly all who heard. Palin had defeated popular three-time incumbent Mayor John Stein by the comfortable margin of 651 to 440 votes. Few had thought it could be done. Wasilla's mayoral race of 1996 was unlike any the city had ever seen, but then Wasilla was unlike anything it had been before, as well.

An astonishing rate of growth had continued to transform the little town throughout Palin's time on the city council. Much of this growth came from the northward migration of North Slope oil workers who chose to base their families in Wasilla, now—with improved roads— nearly a bedroom community to Anchorage. Many of these families were transplants from other oil-producing states like Oklahoma, Texas, and Louisiana. They brought more than oil field expertise with them—most also brought a strong evangelical, Bible Belt–brand of faith and an equally robust political conservatism. These were God-and-country people. Flag fliers. Avid hunters who knew how to field dress a deer and clean a pheasant. They may have been from *outside*, but Palin liked these folks, and they liked her.

Previous mayoral elections had been virtually free of the mention of political parties and of the big issues over which those parties tended to fight. After all, whether or not the gravel airstrip should be paved with concrete or asphalt isn't really an issue that divides folks along party lines. Most Wasillans probably never knew that John Stein was a Republican or that he was moderate to liberal in his political philosophy. Yet by the mid-1990s, Wasilla was a bigger, more Christian, more conservative place, and the shadow of state and national political battles loomed over the area in ways never seen before. For the first time, abortion, gun rights, and the very role and scope of government were topics of discussion as citizens lined up behind their preferred candidates.

In other words, certain cultural and political winds that had been blowing in the Lower 48 for decades finally began to move through the Mat-Su Valley. Some residents were so preoccupied they didn't feel the breeze. But Sarah Palin did.

Although the twentieth century began and ended with the election of a moderate conservative to the White House—William McKinley and George W. Bush—it was inarguably a liberal century. The two Roosevelts, Wilson, Truman, and LBJ all left office only after reshaping the nation in profound and lasting ways. In retrospect, even the former cold-war warrior Nixon pulled the nation leftward, both economically and on the foreign front.

Two significant conservative surges in the last half of the twentieth century interrupted this leftward march. The first swept Ronald Reagan into the White House in 1980. The second, in 1994, put Republicans in control of Congress for the first time in four decades and put Newt Gingrich in the Speaker's chair.

The conventional wisdom tells us that Reagan's victory and the Republican gains in the House and Senate that accompanied it were largely a referendum on Jimmy Carter and his national *malaise*. High interest rates, high inflation, gas rationing, and America's seeming inability to solve a hostage situation in Iran doomed the party in power, according to the prevailing narrative. There is obviously truth in this, yet it ignores a powerful but subtler shift in the political culture—the rise of what would come to be known as *the religious Right*.

If this transforming movement has a birth date, it was January 22, 1973: *Roe v. Wade*. The Supreme Court decision stripping states of the authority to restrict access to abortion in almost any way represents a gigantic watershed moment in American history. Personal opinions about the practice of abortion aside, it is impossible to deny that to this very day, much of the fury, fear, and fanaticism that surround our national elections is a direct outgrowth of the knowledge that the composition of the Supreme Court determines the fate of that 1973 ruling. Only 1857's tragic *Dred Scott v. Sandford* validating slavery had a more polarizing effect on the nation. The Dred Scott decision led inexorably to the War Between the States. Some have described the four-decade electoral and cultural battle over abortion triggered by *Roe v. Wade* as "a war *within* the states."

Churches and Christian ministers led the abolitionist movement in the years after *Dred Scott v. Sandford*. Churches were likewise at the forefront of the pro-life movement that swept the country in the wake of *Roe v. Wade*. Take the Southern Baptists for example.

Prior to 1973, the twelve million or so Southern Baptists in the

United States were overwhelmingly Democratic in their voting patterns. After 1973, Southern Baptists began to leave the party in droves, and that exodus shifted the entire electoral playing field in the southern United States. Only the fact that Jimmy Carter was himself a Southern Baptist and generally perceived to be a cultural conservative kept them in the Democrat fold for the 1976 elections.

Oklahoma provides a perfect illustration of this phenomenon. For every presidential election between 1907 when Oklahoma became a state and 1976, a remarkable pattern held true. The Republican candidate invariably carried counties in which Methodists outnumbered Baptists. Counties that had more Baptists than Methodists were always carried by the Democrats. This was, in part, an echo of the Civil War and the bitter feelings held over from the Reconstruction period. Republican Methodists from Union-supporting Kansas settled in northern and western Oklahoma. The southern and eastern sections of the state saw Baptist settlement from Confederate states like Arkansas and Texas. The Methodist-Baptist balance accurately predicted the presidential voting patterns of all seventy-seven Oklahoma counties for seventy years. Then came 1980.

In the election that took Ronald Reagan into the White House, the Southern Baptists' post–*Roe v. Wade* swing to the Republican Party was fully underway. In many of Oklahoma's Baptist majority counties, voters pulled the lever for a Republican candidate for the first time in their lives, and Reagan carried the state handily. No Democratic presidential candidate has carried Oklahoma since Jimmy Carter—not even the Baptist from neighboring Arkansas, Bill Clinton.

Left-of-center political historians like to attribute the Democrats' loss of the South wholly to latent racism—a reaction to the civil rights movement. The fact is that Democrats lost the South when they lost the Southern Baptists, and the Baptists left the Democratic Party only after deciding the party had long ago left them.

Like a number of other evangelical groups, they began to see the Democrats as hostile to their values on a range of issues important to them—including pornography, homosexuality, and prayer in schools—but most of all, on abortion.

Concurrent with this shift came the rise of Christian media. Christian radio stations and television networks proliferated, providing evangelicals with inspirational teaching or contemporary Christian music as a respite from the increasingly crass fare on mainstream outlets. These became alternative sources of news and commentary as well.

For many, Jerry Falwell became the face of the rising religious Right in the 1980s, along with his Moral Majority organization. But much more influential in the long run were Pat Robertson, utilizing television, and Dr. James Dobson, a family-and-marriage counselor on the radio. Robertson's efforts to inform and mobilize churchgoing Americans through lobbying organizations such as the Freedom Council are well known. He even mounted a run for the presidency in 1988. Other similar but lesser known groups had a huge impact as well. Among them were Tim LaHaye's American Coalition for Traditional Values, Beverly LaHaye's (Tim's wife) Concerned Women for America, and Eagle Forum, founded by 1970s anti-ERA warrior Phyllis Schlafly.

It is James Dobson, founder of a public policy organization called the Family Research Council, who is the figure secular activists most love to hate. In a book titled *Republican Gomorrah: Inside the Movement That Shattered the Party*, anti-Christian crusader Max Blumenthal paints grotesque caricatures of most of the leading figures of the modern evangelical movement, but none is more monstrous than the one he draws of Dobson:

> James Dobson is the quintessential strict father whose influence has been compared by journalistic observers to that of a cult leader. Unlike most of his peers, Dobson had no theological

credentials or religious training. He was a child psychologist who burst onto the scene with a best-selling book that urged beating children into submission in order to restore the respect for God and government that America's youth had lost during the 1960s. Dobson leveraged his fame and wealth to build a kingdom of crisis that counseled the trauma-wracked Middle American masses with Christian-oriented solutions to their personal problems. Then he marshaled them into apocalyptic morality crusades against abortion and homosexuality.[2]

No person familiar with Dobson's Focus on the Family radio ministry or with the man himself will find traces of the grandfatherly humanitarian they know in Blumenthal's portrait. In reality, Dobson was utterly nonpolitical prior to 1986, and Focus on the Family rarely dealt with any topic other than Christian parenting or marriage. Through the late 1970s and early 1980s, Dobson's radio program and child-rearing books made him one of the most beloved and trusted personalities in all of broadcasting—Christian or secular. Millions of parents across North America benefited from his counsel on topics such as handling a strong-willed child. Dobson was and is an advocate of spanking, but only within tightly constrained parameters and never in anger, Blumenthal's reference to "beating children into submission" to the contrary.

Then, in 1985, President Reagan's attorney general, Edwin Meese, approached Dobson about participating in a blue ribbon commission charged with investigating and reporting on the possible negative impacts of pornography in society. Specifically, the group was to explore the question of whether there is a link between pornography consumption and violence or criminal behavior. The Meese Commission, as it came to be called, was chaired by Federal Judge Henry Hudson and had members drawn from a variety of fields, including psychiatry and law enforcement.

Dobson resisted at first, but eventually agreed to serve. What he saw and heard in the course of the commission's investigation broke his heart and transformed his sense of calling. Furthermore, the relentless attacks from the political and cultural Left that he and his fellow panelists endured before they had even submitted their report forced him into the political battle to defend the commission's honor and the integrity of its findings.

The scarred and battle-hardened Dobson that emerged from the ordeal was a reluctant but formidable culture warrior. Not long after this experience, he refocused his educational nonprofit, the Family Research Council, raised significant sums of money from like-minded donors, and began mobilizing grassroots support around issues and elections.

With the advent of the Internet and e-mail, organizations like the Family Research Council, Robertson's Christian Coalition, and LaHaye's Concerned Women for America could reach the remotest places and activate church- and community-based networks instantly and at little cost. This included largely isolated locations like the Mat-Su Valley of Alaska, where evangelical churches were increasing in number and where evangelical influence was being newly felt in the politics of Wasilla. Once people on both sides of the debate started caring passionately about how their presidents, senators, congressmen, and governors stood on issues like abortion and pornography, it became unreasonable to think they were going to stop caring about these matters when it came to mayoral races.

Palin's church membership, diverse circles of friends, and her tendency to mix and mingle with a wide variety of Wasillans put her in touch with that reality. Her non-evangelical opponent never saw it coming.

Palin's election as mayor came two years after the famed Gingrich-led conservative revolution of 1994. It was an election in which many Americans expressed alarm about the leftward shift the country seemed to be taking in Bill Clinton's first year and a half in office, especially after Hillary Clinton's failed attempt to remake the nation's health care system in a more European mold. Gingrich had helped organize a slate of congressional candidates running on a conservative platform labeled "A Contract With America." The policy road map had been cowritten with Texans Tom DeLay and Richard Armey and with significant inspiration from Ronald Reagan's 1985 State of the Union address. It worked. It was wildly popular among conservatives and equally successful politically.

Palin's little Wasilla mayoral campaign took its cues from Republican success in the Lower 48. She made no effort to conceal her pro-life views, her robust support of gun owners' rights, and most of all her Reagan-esque conviction that the government that governs least, governs best.

Some Wasillans were offended to see abortion politics introduced in a place that didn't even have its own hospital. Understandably, people who are ambivalent about the issue of abortion prefer to see the unpleasant topic avoided altogether. Yet for voters who have strong convictions about the practice—who see it not only as a moral dilemma but also a civil and human rights issue—it is absolutely relevant when assessing a candidate.

In fact, years later, this very reality put Sarah in a painful family dilemma at the end of her second term as mayor. A term limits measure enacted before Sarah became mayor meant she would have to step down at the end of her second three-year term. As she launched a statewide run for the office of lieutenant governor, her mother-in-law, Faye Palin, surprised many—Sarah among them—by deciding to run to replace her as mayor of Wasilla. Like a number of Sarah's good friends in the community, including some of her Elite Six buddies, Faye Palin held pro-abortion rights views.

Her mother-in-law's candidacy put Sarah in a profoundly awkward position. She loved Todd's parents and treasured her relationship with them. At the same time, Sarah is hardwired to be unshakably principle driven, and, on those principles, she had run two campaigns for mayor declaring that Wasilla's leader should be pro-life. Furthermore, she was in the middle of a statewide race in which she was trumpeting her pro-life views. To make matters worse, Sarah had real concerns about Faye's electability. There were rumors that Sarah's nemesis, John Stein, was considering another run for mayor as a Democrat. The competitive fighter in her hated the thought of Stein and company winning and reversing the direction of the city. Then, too, a public endorsement of Faye Palin would have left Sarah open to a charge of nepotism or perhaps of trying to establish a family dynasty in Wasilla.

The prudent course was obviously to remain neutral in the race, but her determination to see Stein kept out of City Hall got the best of her. In a move she would later regret, Sarah quietly recruited a friend who shared her ideological bent to run for the open mayor's seat. As she relates in *Going Rogue*, when Todd found out about it, he was angry and hurt.

The move caused short-term damage to Sarah's relationship with her husband and longer lasting wounds with her in-laws.

> It was a nasty brew, mixing local politics, which is notoriously contentious, with family politics.... The truth was, I had let the heat of politics get in the way of family. Faye would never have done that to me. In fact, even though we disagree on some issues, when I later ran for VP, she worked incredibly hard for John McCain and me, traveling around the nation to campaign for us. She and Jim helped lead successful efforts in some western states. But that's what politics can do to you if you don't catch yourself: the heat of battle causes a little core of self-centeredness to harden in your heart, so subtly that you're not even aware of it.[3]

Of course, all of this lay far in the future on the day Sarah took the reins of city government in Wasilla a few weeks after the election of 1994.

In the competitive worlds of sports and business, it is common for a new coach or a new CEO to clean house and bring in his or her own staff upon taking the helm. Indeed, most experienced corporate managers insist on it. In her first few months as mayor of Wasilla, Palin found out why.

Upon taking office, she had initially left all city department heads in place despite the fact that it was clearly within her powers to replace them. Her reasoning was that they had a lot of valuable experience, a treasury of wisdom she knew she would need. She soon discovered, though, that this longevity can engender more than just expertise. Some of her department heads were entrenched, invested in the status quo, and still loyal to Palin's predecessor, nine-year Mayor John Stein and his allies, like Nick Carney. In fact, the entire group had signed a newspaper ad endorsing Stein during the election and had campaigned for him in various ways—some subtle, some overt. Once Palin became mayor, many of these same department heads resisted her leadership, often in the passive-aggressive manner that bureaucrats often employ.

Tensions mounted and tempers flared. Finally, recognizing that each of these job posts was a political appointment by design and that the holders served at the pleasure of the sitting mayor, Palin requested letters of resignation from all the department heads. These would be kept on file and only retrieved and accepted if Palin found that city employee unwilling or unable to work constructively with her.

This proved to be the case with Irl Stambaugh, the chief of police. She had instructed all city department heads to submit a contingency plan for cutting their budgets should cuts become necessary. Stambaugh flatly refused to comply, and Palin eventually fired him. Stunned and humiliated, the ex-police chief sued Palin and the city for wrongful termination based on an allegation of sexual discrimination. His assertion was that Palin, as a woman, was too fragile to deal with a strong, opinionated man like himself and that she was excessively intimidated by him.

This accusation tended to produce howls of laughter among long-time Wasillans who knew Sarah Palin. The loudest laughter came from her father, her brother, and her husband. The girl who had worked the fishing grounds off Bristol Bay and the locker rooms of the sports beat in Anchorage had been living and working in male-dominated worlds all of her life. Whatever Stambaugh's firing was, it wasn't sexual discrimination! A judge soon agreed. He threw the case out of court, acknowledging that the chief of police serves at the pleasure of the mayor, and required Stambaugh to reimburse the city for its legal expenses in the case. It was the kind of early victory that gave many Wasillans new confidence in their young, intrepid mayor.

Some Wasillans were harder to win over. The local paper, the *Mat-Su Valley Frontiersman*, was dubious about Palin in those rough opening months of her administration. She soon won the paper over, though, and was delighted when once skeptical editorial writers eventually came to laud her performance through two terms of rapid change in the valley.

What Palin consistently demonstrated in her tenure was a forward-looking commitment to building infrastructure like paved roads and sewer lines, a fierce drive to keep the tax and regulatory burden on both individuals and businesses to an absolute minimum, and a deep empathy for common, working families—the people some derisively label *Wal-Mart Americans*. These principles she celebrated under the banner of a political philosophy she would repeatedly describe as *common sense conservatism*. It was a theme that had resonated with the residents of the Mat-Su Valley, and Palin knew she was fashioning her own version of a political brand, one that she hoped might reach to a wider electorate.

Chapter 9

THE PALIN POLITICAL BRAND

Common sense is genius dressed in its working clothes.
—RALPH WALDO EMERSON

DURING HER YEARS IN WASILLA POLITICS, SARAH PALIN evolved what would become her political brand. It was a blend of values, policies, and personality that proved popular at the time and that opened even greater opportunities for her in the years to come. This blend was admittedly informal, unapologetically simple, and seemingly just right for the times. Yet its very informality could cause it to be overlooked, and so it is important to consider its sources before moving forward with her journey through Alaska politics.

She had been a unique creature on the political landscape of Alaska, as she would be on the broader national stage. Though she had studied journalism in college and had entered politics almost accidentally, she became an unswerving advocate of conservative values, a bold champion of an almost libertarian worldview. Opponents were stunned and supporters were delighted, but few knew where Palin's full-bodied philosophy found its source or how she came to hold her views with such fiery reverence. They did not know that Palin's views had evolved much as they do in the lives of most Americans—not from the university or a learned mentor or formal immersion in a body of truths—but from the informal pastiche of influences that shapes most political behavior—that best of all teachers called *life*.

If the modern conservative movement has a specific date of inception, it is the day in 1951 on which William F. Buckley's book *God and Man at Yale* was released. Buckley had just graduated from Yale with honors and had decided that much that was wrong with his education was producing what was wrong with America. In time, Buckley would write that he and his philosophical fellows were destined to stand athwart the course of the twentieth century and shout, "Stop."[1] And so they did, but only because they first stood upon the shoulders of giants from an earlier generation.

When these conservative fathers and mothers were asked which books most shaped their worldviews, often the same books emerged in their answers again and again. Contemporary conservative writer Jonah Goldberg has called these books "the conservative canon." High on this list are works like Friedrich Von Hayek's *The Road to Serfdom*, Leo Strauss's *The City and Man*, and Adam Smith's *The Wealth of Nations*. Buckley himself was widely influential, not least for his founding of the magazine *National Review*. So were key contemporaries of Buckley's such as Russell Kirk (*The Conservative Mind*), intellectual anticommunists like Jeane Kirkpatrick (*The Strategy of Deception*), and Whittaker Chambers (*Witness*). A third generation of conservative intellectuals in America includes University of Chicago professor Allan Bloom (*The Closing of the American Mind*), Judge Robert Bork (*Slouching Towards Gomorrah*), and Thomas Sowell (*A Conflict of Visions*).

Among the current crop of conservative thought leaders there is a subgroup that merits special mention. A number of individuals who were leftist radicals or left-leaning socialists during the turbulent

1960s, many of them Jewish, ultimately became disillusioned with Marxism and came to believe that not only was socialism as a system fatally flawed, but it was also a threat to freedom and human dignity. Many of the writings mentioned above provided an intellectual road map for these former liberals. Because they were *newly* converted to the conservative cause, some unhappy liberals began to call these individuals *neoconservatives* or, more simply, *neocons*.

During the Bush administration, these neocons became the favorite bogeymen of the American Left and the conspiracy-minded Far Right. Indeed, in some quarters the epithet *neocon* has become a thin veneer for anti-Semitism, belief in Jewish or Israeli conspiracy theories, and murmurings about excessive Jewish influence on the media.

Among the occasional targets of such ugly whispers are *New York Times* columnist David Brooks and former George W. Bush speech-writer David Frum. Both men are intelligent, patriotic, graduates of top-tier universities, and steeped in the writings of the conservative canon. Both men are Jewish.

It might seem natural that these men would welcome Sarah Palin and her earthy brand of conservatism. It might seem fitting that, given the opposition they have endured for their views, these men might have had the broad-mindedness to recognize the big tent of American conservatism and to offer Palin a place within. Sadly, this has been far from true. In fact, both men have been sharply critical of Palin, and in doing so they have belied much of what they claim to believe.

A few weeks before the 2008 presidential election, Brooks wrote:

> In America, there has always been a separate, populist, strain. For those in this school, book knowledge is suspect but practical knowledge is respected. The city is corrupting and the univer-sities are kindergartens for overeducated fools.... This populist tendency produced the term-limits movement based on the

belief that time in government destroys character but contact with grass-roots America gives one grounding in real life. And now it has produced Sarah Palin.[2]

In a 2008 interview with *The Atlantic* magazine's Jeffrey Goldberg, Brooks said Palin's nonintellectual, nonelitist populism "represents a fatal cancer to the Republican Party."[3] A clue to what Brooks may be looking for in a candidate can be found in some of his praise for Barack Obama. In the same interview in which he referred to Palin as a cancer, he related a conversation he had late one night with a weary Senator Obama. Brooks asked the young Illinois senator if he was familiar with any of the writings of Reinhold Niebuhr. When Obama said yes, Brooks asked him what Niebuhr meant to him:

> For the next 20 minutes, he gave me a perfect description of Reinhold Niebuhr's thought, which is a very subtle thought process based on the idea that you have to use power while it corrupts you. And I was dazzled, I felt the tingle up my knee as Chris Matthews would say.[4]

Clearly, Brooks and his like-minded peers prefer intellectuals, first principles aside, and so it is not hard to discern why they would look askance at Sarah Palin. She has an accent that reminds a New England elitist of the uneducated and the blue-collar Midwest. She has stumbled over historical and policy questions in interviews and seems uninterested and unengaged in intellectual pursuits. Nor is it likely that she has read Niebuhr, Hayek, Buckley, or Bloom. And yet she has come to hold most of the same policy convictions as these conservative intellectuals and to give these principles her full-throated support. How can this be so?

The answer goes to the root of what Palin means by "common sense conservatism." It is a conservatism that is reached via a strong internal moral compass and an unapologetic embrace of America's

Puritan and Calvinist heritage. It is visceral rather than cerebral, yet it leads to very much the same place.

Though Bill Buckley was an East Coast, Ivy League intellectual, he had a savvy appreciation for this kind of gut-level conservatism and the drawbacks of an elite education. He once famously said, "I am obliged to confess I should sooner live in a society governed by the first two thousand names in the Boston telephone directory than in a society governed by the two thousand faculty members of Harvard University."[5]

Fifty-five years before Peggy Noonan referred to Palin as "out of her depth in a shallow pool,"[6] or Danielle Crittenden (David Frum's wife) said, "Palin's undisciplined and inane rambling needs to be euthanized like a race horse with a broken leg,"[7] Bill Buckley, in the inaugural issue of *National Review*, gave a prescient description of Palin's plight when he wrote: "Radical conservatives in this country have an interesting time of it, for when they are not being suppressed or mutilated by Liberals, they are being ignored or humiliated by a great many of those of the well-fed Right."[8]

What seems to bother many on "the well-fed Right" is that Palin's common sense conservatism was not forged through wrestling with meaty concepts like Locke's theory of the social compact, but it was simply born of a sense of what is right and fair, of a grasp of core American values. It is a conservatism absorbed not so much through philosophy but by observation, not so much through books but by viewing the world through a biblical and patriotic American lens. This is what has landed Palin where she is politically, and it ought not be despised but rather welcomed by those who fight for traditional Americanism in the contentious public square.

There is a sense in which life teaches conservatism naturally, and thus conservatives have only to affirm what is obvious in order to make their case. Americans listen to Rush Limbaugh not to be told what to think but rather because he offers them a validating case for what they already know in their guts to be right. Limbaugh reads *National Review* and the *Weekly Standard* and distills the arguments for people too busy trying to bootstrap a business or working that extra job so they can get the orthodontist paid. They tune in to Hugh Hewitt, Michael Medved, or Sean Hannity for affirmation of their instinct. They have not read Allan Bloom's observations on "the Nietzscheanization of the Left."[9] They have not read the canon of Russell Kirk. Yet they have sat in church, they have heard the old men declaim on the benches of the town square, and they have seen what works in the world around them. Conservatism for them is simply the way of the wise, what life teaches to those who have ears to hear.

These visceral conservatives have a fundamental sense of morality that tells them it is unfair and unwise for their government to confiscate large chunks of what they produce by the sweat of their brows only to have it squandered on silly bureaucracies or handed over to slackers, underachievers, and trial lawyers. They may not know Adam Smith from Adam, but they know that what Paul Harvey used to say on their radios about the power of the free enterprise system still makes sense to them. They may not be able to make a case for natural law in a debate, but their moral instincts and daily choices give it a greater affirmation than any orator possibly could.

This is the animating impulse of the Tea Party movement. Comprised of Republicans, Independents, and, according to some surveys, 16 percent Democrats,[10] this movement is a broad coalition of Americans who are wearied of mounting taxes, afraid of an encroaching state, and determined that their children will not become the slaves of the socialist dream. These are the pillars of common sense conservatism, and if there is no place at the table of public service for Sarah Palin and the vast swaths of Americans who cling to these pillars, then the would-be thought leaders of the conservative movement will surely find themselves at the head of a poorer, sparser parade.

Sarah Palin's political worldview was drawn from many informal sources, and in this she is much like the majority of Americans who fashion their worldviews from truths life presses upon them. There was, for example, the influence of Paul Harvey. Intellectuals will scoff, but for three generations of Americans, Paul Harvey was the only political education required. In the Heath home, the published collections of Harvey's *The Rest of the Story* radio transcripts were cherished, read aloud, much discussed, and often debated. Indeed, it was not uncommon for one of the Heath children to end a semi-serious lecture to the family with Harvey's famous words, "...and now you know the rest of the story."

A classic example of Paul Harvey's instructive artistry is an economics object lesson he repeated many times throughout his five decades on American radios. It begins with the jarring declaration, "The pilgrim fathers of the United States were communists." Harvey goes on to describe how the first Massachusetts colonists under Governor Bradford began their farming operations as a commune—laboring together on a common plot of land—and how they almost starved to death. Only when these Pilgrims switched to a system of private farming did productivity soar, thus leading to the first Thanksgiving.

Harvey finished this historical parable with the words, "The communist experiment in America—as with all communist experiments, past, present, and future—was foredoomed to failure."[11]

In these and hundreds of Paul Harvey broadcast lessons, Sarah Palin found the raw material of her budding worldview. She was already a Christian and already believed that there was a moral order to the universe. Harvey connected that moral order—a faith-based order he too held dear—to the events of the day. Young Sarah and many in her generation like her learned from Harvey that history is a vital mentor, that the power of the state must always be contained if freedom is to thrive, that only daring men and women build great societies, and that faith and optimism are essential to a meaningful life. As Harvey often said, "In times like these, it helps to recall that there have always been times like these."[12]

That the political philosophy of a modern politician could have her worldview shaped, in part, by a radio broadcaster will give some intellectuals and conservative elites reason to laugh with disdain. Yet these same thinkers will argue against their liberal opponents by insisting that conservatism is common sense, that it screams its truth from the marketplace almost literally, and that only bias allows an objective reader to miss its lessons on the pages of history. In other words, they will contend that conservative principles are simple, easy to understand, yet powerful in their impact. Paul Harvey would have agreed. So would Sarah Palin. And this is why a bookish girl in a small town in Alaska could become a conservative, in part, because she has absorbed the conservative philosophy of the most successful broadcaster of her generation.

She could also easily become a conservative through her devotion to reading. As we have seen, books were almost as numerous as animal pelts in the Palin home, and they were oft read and much cherished. Sarah, in particular, read all she could, and this is what brought her to one of the greatest influences upon her life: C. S. Lewis. In the famed Christian apologist and Oxford don she found arguments that allowed her to synthesize and harmonize the two halves of her life represented by her parents—the science and empiricism of her father and the mystical faith of her mother.

She devoured Lewis's fiction, such as the revered The Chronicles of Narnia series, but did not hesitate to dive into his meatier works as well. *Mere Christianity* and *Miracles* were among her favorites, as they were for several generations of college-bound Christians who have found that these intellectual defenses of Christianity answered the faith-corroding environment of the public university.

Perhaps most significant to the formation of Sarah's religious worldview was Lewis's cultural critique *The Abolition of Man*. *National Review*, the flagship publication of the conservative movement in America, ranked *The Abolition of Man* number seven on its "100 Best Non-Fiction Books of the Century list."[13] In it Lewis anticipates postmodern moral relativism and the use of science as a basis for debunking all objective systems of moral values. He defends and upholds the validity of science but warns that without the restraining, humanizing, and civilizing role of moral truth, science becomes a threat to freedom.

One of the most influential and widely quoted chapters from *Abolition* is titled "Men Without Chests." The premise of the section is a metaphor in which humans are three-part creatures—the head (intellect) on top, the stomach (appetites) at the bottom, and in between, the chest (the repository of faith, compassion, and character) mediating between and elevating the other two. It is a devastating critique of the two ascendant trends of our day—nihilistic hedonism on the one hand (stomach people) or atheistic rationalism on the other (head people).

Lewis observed that those who build a culture on intellect and appetite alone *want* the vital virtues of *chest* but categorically reject the moral codes and moral accountability necessary to create them. He wrote that the educators and leaders of such a time "make men without chests and expect of them virtue and enterprise. We laugh at honour and are shocked to find traitors in our midst. We castrate and bid the geldings be fruitful."[14] It was the kind of language that would embed itself in the soul of a bright, introspective high school student and that would surface years later in the politics of a rising conservative star.

By the time Sarah stepped into local Wasilla politics, she had already been shaped by a number of intellectual forces that are easy to underestimate but that had profound influence upon her life. First was the biblical faith she acquired from her mother, from her church, and from the devoted Christian ministers in her life, like Paul Riley and Theron Horne. In her experience, Scripture was not merely a handbook on relating to God; it was a system of truth that applied to every area of life, the foundational principles for approaching and understanding the doings of mankind. This carried with it a political philosophy all its own. Sarah would know, for example, that there are sluggards in the world and that no amount of aid will make a difference to this sort. She would know too that if a man won't work, he should not eat. She would also understand that moral conduct is essential to great leadership, as it is to nations, and that to assure this morality it is necessary to have boundaries, safeguards, and restraints. All of this would have been obvious to her before her first day on the Wasilla City Council.

Beyond the Bible and C. S. Lewis, Sarah had also read the great works of the American experience. She had a good memory, particularly for potent, pithy statements, and so she would carry with her all her life such founding wisdom as "that government governs best which governs least" or "the power to tax is the power to destroy." These principles of American origins lived in her. During much of her Alaskan political life she would carry a copy of the state constitution. This made sense to her friends who understood that she loves words and lives by them, that the journalist in her revels in language as a guide to life.

Yet after all of her young intellectual preparation, it was her simple observation of life as it was that convinced her of the principles upon which she would build her political career. She saw the good that government could do in assuring the general welfare. She loved seeing good roads or new schools change a community. Nearly her first political act was creating a police force to make her community safe. Yet she also saw what political power put at the behest of the greedy and the domineering could mean. She knew instinctively that power draws human beings of low character, the grasping and the cheats. She concluded early that a libertarian society was best, one in which government was limited so that no special interest could capture its power for ill use. Such a society would guarantee freedom for all, opportunity for all, yet without assuring equality of results. Men would rise to their best and create for generations yet to come. Government would simply assure a level playing field and the protections necessary for a valiant people to thrive.

This became the Palin political brand. It was a politic that allowed the government of Wasilla to do what it did best—public works, law enforcement, protection of the free market, order and safety for all citizens. Yet what Palin fought was government as a tool of the few, as a means of profit for the sly and the scheming. This is what she opposed, and this is what brought her into conflict with men like Stein, Stambaugh, and Carney, men who thought public service meant privilege and benefits for the elite.

By the time Sarah was finishing her term as mayor of Wasilla, her brand of tempered, benevolent libertarianism had become wildly popular in her region and was already causing some supporters to urge her on to bigger things. And those things would come, but not before Palin's political philosophy was tested and refined in the furnace of Alaskan politics.

Chapter 10

"IF I DIE, I DIE"

*Our minds tell us, and history confirms, that the great
threat to freedom is the concentration of power....Even
though the men who wield this power initially be of good
will and even though they be not corrupted by the power
they exercise, the power will both attract and form men of
a different stamp.*[1]

—MILTON FRIEDMAN
Capitalism and Freedom

A S THE YOUNGEST PERSON AND FIRST WOMAN EVER ELECTED
governor of Alaska, Sarah Palin was on top of the world.
Literally.

Speaking to a group in Barrow, Alaska, on May 4, 2007, she
was three hundred thirty miles north of the Arctic Circle and in
the northernmost inhabited point in the United States. Spring had
arrived at the North Slope. The thermometer would peak that sunny
Friday at a balmy fourteen degrees above zero. She was in her fifth
month in office.

Back in Juneau, eleven hundred miles away, Bill McAllister, the
capital reporter for Anchorage's NBC affiliate KTUU, was among
several reporters frantically trying to reach the governor or a staff
member by phone. In mid-2007, cellular signal coverage had not yet

found its way that close to the North Pole. All were hoping to be the first reporter to get the governor's reaction to the huge breaking news story of the day. The problem was that due to the isolation of Barrow, the governor hadn't yet heard about it.

Someone eventually acquired the number of a hard-line telephone near where the governor was giving her speech and managed to get Palin herself on the line. The reporter dropped the bombshell news. Two former Republican state legislators, one of them former Speaker of the House Peter Kott, and a current Republican legislator had all just been arrested in a federal corruption probe. The primary charges against the three centered on allegations of soliciting and receiving illegal money and favors from one of the state's largest oil and gas production services companies, the VECO Corporation.

A little later on in the day, McAllister begged the governor for a commitment to meet him for an on-camera interview after she got back to the state capital that evening. It was a lot to ask. The governor had been on the move since before dawn, and the flight back to Juneau was the equivalent of traveling from Dallas to Washington DC in a small aircraft. But it was a massive story, and the governor agreed.

McAllister walked up from the press office in the capitol basement around nine thirty that night and made his way through the corridors. The offices were largely empty and dark. The state legislators and their staffs had long since headed for their favored Juneau watering holes. They had much to talk about this evening. Three of their own had been led away in handcuffs earlier in the day, and rumors were swirling that there were more arrests to come.

Television station KTUU's designated spot for shooting stand-up reports and interviews from the capitol happened to be on the second floor, right outside the speaker's chambers. As McAllister topped the stairs and rounded the corner, he found the familiar hallway cavernous and still. Soon he saw a figure sitting on one of the hallway benches just outside the locked speaker's chambers.

It was the governor, with five-year-old Piper asleep in her arms. No entourage. No handlers. Simply there to fulfill a promise. Thirty-five minutes later, Palin did a live interview for the 10:00 p.m. news in Anchorage while her daughter slept on the bench a few yards away. The moment impressed McAllister. It was a rare display of integrity and grace by a politician that the hardened reporter would never forget. It was particularly remarkable given the political circumstances then unfolding.

Palin's statements that night to McAllister and throughout the unfolding events were consistent and firm. As a fiercely proud Alaskan, the arrests and the ugly national headlines they generated embarrassed her. As a Republican, the systemic corruption they exposed outraged her. But the incident also served to vindicate the entire premise of her successful campaign for the governor's office. She had run, not within the Republican Party power structure in Alaska, but outside of it. Indeed, she'd run in spite of it: even against it.

What Palin said was true. For two years she had been railing against a set of backroom political manipulators and the deals they had struck with a handful of major oil companies. She was convinced these deals were disastrously bad for the people of Alaska. Understanding why she thought so and how her crusade against corruption propelled her to the governor's mansion reveals much about her and much about the political culture in which we live.

Owning a piece of land—nothing is more fundamentally infused in the American ethos or linked to the American dream. Yet in Alaska, the largest piece of undeveloped land in the United States, the federal government owns nearly 60 percent of the vast acreage, the state controls another 28 percent, and native peoples have most of the remaining 12 percent. In reality, less than 1 percent of Alaska's 658,000 resource-rich square miles is citizen-owned.[2]

This has produced a unique set of circumstances there. And a unique mind-set to match.

The mineral wealth of Alaska is staggering to contemplate. Gold brought the state to the attention of the world in the 1890s. In the years since, silver, copper, tin, and coal have been found in abundance there too. Above the ground, vast timber forests stretch from horizon to horizon.

In the gasoline-thirsty twentieth century, however, it was oil that defined Alaska's wealth potential. It had been known for decades that there was abundant oil to be had in Alaska, particularly in the Kenai Peninsula south of Anchorage. The challenge was getting the extracted crude to refineries in the Lower 48. Then in 1968, vast repositories of oil were discovered under the permafrost of the North Slope at the very northern edge of the state. Immediately, proposals to build a pipeline connecting the North Slope to sea-based shipping in the south emerged, but they were met with fierce resistance from environmentalists and Alaska Native groups. Lawsuits and legal filings delayed action for years, but amid the OPEC oil embargo and gas shortages of the early 1970s, the nation became eager to see those reserves developed. The result was federal legislation green-lighting one of the most ambitious engineering undertakings since the constructing of the Panama Canal—the Trans-Alaska Pipeline, which would carry crude oil from Prudhoe Bay at the top of the state to the Valdez Terminals on Prince William Sound, some eight hundred miles to the south.

The pipeline was completed in 1977 with private funds from a consortium of three of the major oil companies of the day—British Petroleum, ARCO, and Humble Oil. They would recoup their costs in profits from their own oil production on the slope and by charging other oil companies a fee to move their oil through the pipeline. It sounded like a feasible arrangement, but in practice those fees ended up discouraging other oil companies from developing their North Slope holdings because they took too big a bite out of profit margins—especially when oil prices were low.

Decades later, many knowledgeable Alaskans would warn state leaders against repeating that same mistake when a new pipeline proposal was dominating political discussions in the state. Nevertheless, the Trans-Alaska Pipeline transformed Alaska economically. Taxes on oil profits and shipping, as well as royalties from oil production on state lands, flooded state coffers, allowing the state to slash the tax burden on individual citizens. Before the pipeline, Alaska's state income tax rate was 14.5 percent—the highest in the nation.[3] The inescapable logic of mathematics drove the high tax rate. Alaska had a tiny population, spread across staggering distances, in a brand-new state that had little infrastructure in place. It had challenges no other state had ever faced—expensive challenges.

Completion of the pipeline allowed Alaska to eliminate the state income tax completely. Around the same time, the state established something called the Alaska Permanent Fund. The fund was written into the very constitution of the state by amendment and called for 25 percent of certain oil-and-gas-related revenues to be set aside in a sort of endowment for the people of Alaska.[4]

The driving philosophy behind the Permanent Fund was a simple one. It recognized that though individual Alaskans had only a tiny sliver of the state available for private ownership, and even less where mineral rights are available, the state's natural resource wealth belonged to all Alaskans collectively, and it was therefore a moral imperative that all Alaskans benefit from the development of those resources.

The fund grew rapidly through deposits from the state, and it grew further still through prudent investment of the capital. As a result, each year every citizen of Alaska receives a dividend check from the fund. The size of that check varies and is calculated using a set formula—one based upon the fund's average income in the previous five years. In 2009 that dividend check was $1,305 to every man, woman, and child who had lived in the state the entirety of the previous year. The payout totaled $875 million. The year before it was $2,069. What is more, Governor Palin gained approval for her "Alaska's Clear and Equitable Share" (ACES) measure in 2007. This "resource debate" added an additional $1,200 per citizen to the dividend. Thus a family of five in 2008 received checks totaling $16,345.[5]

Understandably, the Permanent Fund has become a significant source of income for Alaska's citizens and therefore a key driver of the state economy. The same is true for the government as a whole. The revised 2010 budget forecast for Alaska anticipates that oil taxes, royalties, and fees will provide 82 percent of the state's anticipated $3.18 billion in unrestricted revenues.[6] Add to all that the jobs the industry generates directly and indirectly, and one begins to understand how intricately enmeshed the oil and gas industry has become in the economic life of every Alaskan.

Naturally, the overwhelming majority of Alaskans value the presence of the oil industry in their state. Though most are staunch conservationists, they have seen with their own eyes that development of natural resources and preservation of nature are not mutually exclusive. Three decades later, almost none of the doomsday predictions from opponents of the pipeline have materialized, even after a 2002 earthquake that registered 7.9 on the Richter scale. Though not directly related to the pipeline, the 1989 wreck of the *Exxon Valdez* oil tanker in Prince William Sound did deal a temporary blow to the state's confidence.

Still, Alaska is much more like Texas than California in citizen attitudes toward the oil industry. In the Golden State, most citizens oppose development of the state's oil deposits. In Alaska, the vast majority of citizens want the oil and gas industry working in the state, and they would like to see more exploration and drilling, not less.

It is revealing that in a survey conducted ten years after the *Exxon Valdez* tanker spill, 95 percent of Alaskans rated their opinion of oil and gas development in Alaska as "good" or "very good."[7]

Nevertheless, by the turn of the millennium a confluence of events threatened Alaska's oil-driven prosperity. Environmentalists and their allies in Congress had continued their success in keeping a small section of the Arctic National Wildlife Refuge (ANWR) and that section's five to fifteen billion barrels of recoverable oil locked up from exploration. Meanwhile, production was steadily declining on the North Slope for a number of economic reasons, just one of which was the fact that oil was falling out of favor as an energy source due to global concerns about climate change. It became clear to Alaska's leaders that, should these trends continue, all Alaskans would be feeling the negative impacts in a few years.

There was one major good news–bad news element in all of this. The good news was that the North Slope was holding more than oil. It also happens to be one of the largest repositories of natural gas on the planet. And cleaner-burning gas is much less fraught with controversy as an energy source than the derivatives of crude oil.

The bad news was that would-be producers were faced with the same huge challenge they faced with North Slope oil in the early seventies—getting it to market. Efforts to get a natural gas pipeline built go all the way back to the Carter administration. Various proposals have generally fallen into one of two basic strategies for getting natural gas to the Lower 48.

Some have called for building a parallel pipeline that follows the existing route of the Trans-Alaska Pipeline to Valdez. There the gas would be converted to a denser liquid form (LNG) and loaded on ships for transport. Another breed of past proposals has called for building a line that runs southeast to Canada to connect with new or existing pipeline networks there.

What is clear is that since the completion of the Trans-Alaska Pipeline back in 1977, getting a companion natural gas conduit planned, approved, financed, and built has been the elusive holy grail of every successive Alaskan governor. It is an unspeakably complex goal.

Success meant negotiating a labyrinth of existing federal regulations and prohibitions, overcoming court challenges from various opposition groups, and balancing the needs of key interests. There were two key parties occupying the opposite ends of that balancing act. On one side there were the three oil companies with the largest holdings on the North Slope, known as *the Big Three*, for it was mostly likely one or a combination of these that would finance, engineer, and profit from the pipeline. On the other side were the people of Alaska.

In 2002, Alaskans thought they finally had the person who could get it done. The twenty-two-year veteran of the U.S. Senate, Frank Murkowski, had come home to run for governor.

Toward the end of 2001, Palin's second term as Wasilla's mayor entered its final year. The local term limits law meant Sarah was facing a decision about life beyond the mayor's office. She knew she could return to being a full-time mom. This had its appeal, particularly with Piper's addition to the family earlier that year. But Palin took seriously that sense of *calling* to the realm of public policy and government she had first felt those years ago. She began to ponder what her next step might be, how God might cause her path to unfold.

She briefly pondered a run for a seat in the state legislature but quickly rejected that option. Palin knew herself well enough to realize she was ill suited to the deal making, horse trading, and compromise required to be an effective legislator. She saw things in black-and-white terms and knew that lawmaking is done in a sea of gray. She was wired to be an executive, and she knew it.

It was already public knowledge that Alaska's longtime junior U.S. senator, Frank Murkowski, was planning to return from Washington to run for governor. That meant the Republicans would already be geared up to mount a strong statewide effort in the general election.

For five years, Sarah had been the chief executive of the fastest-growing city in Alaska. The majority opinion was that she had performed wonderfully. One of the paradoxes of Alaska is that its *big* places are small and its *little* places enormous. Wasilla is a small town by almost anyone's standard, yet it is Alaska's fourth-largest municipality—prominent and conspicuous. The Mat-Su Borough, home to fewer than sixty thousand souls, is the same physical size as West Virginia. Sarah's accomplishments had been impressive indeed. Palin was a successful, popular mayor, and the state Republican Party establishment had taken note. Frank Murkowski was among those paying attention. Many believed she was destined for big things. So only a few eyebrows rose when she announced herself as a candidate for lieutenant governor.

It was not a wise move. Though Palin initially had a good chance to win, three other Republicans soon announced for the same position, and this gave Sarah heavier competition than she had envisioned. She did her best to juggle motherhood, her full-time responsibilities as mayor, the rigors of a statewide primary campaign, and the fund-raising it demanded. Though she relished the part of campaigning that involved meeting other Alaskans and sharing their love for the state, she had long hated asking for money from potential donors. Thus, she rarely did. As a result, she was vastly outspent by the other leading candidate, State Senate Majority Leader Loren Leman. Still, in the closing weeks of the race, polls showed Palin and Leman in a statistical dead heat.

A few days before the primary election, however, an anonymous sender delivered a set of documents to reporters all over Alaska. These were copies of court records that seemed to indicate that Palin had been charged with a felony fishing violation in 1993. It was big news in papers and newscasts across the state.

There was just one problem. It wasn't accurate.

In that year, Sarah's first on the city council, she had joined Todd and the rest of the Palin clan on the Bristol Bay fishing grounds. She remembers that fishing season well because at one point she was reaching for the side of a fishing skiff as it came alongside a large *tender boat* to which Todd planned to offload his catch. Her hand became trapped between the two boats, smashing four of her fingers. X-rays revealed that no bones were broken, so, bandaged and chastened, she returned to the skiff the next day.

In that same season, she was written up by an Alaska Fish and Game Department official for failing to register as a gillnet permit holder. She was properly registered as a *crew member* on one of the Palin family skiffs, but she had taken over the permit of one of Todd's sisters. That change needed to be registered, but in the rush to catch fish, no one remembered to do it. Sarah received what is essentially the equivalent of a traffic ticket—a misdemeanor violation—yet for some reason the document sent to the media listed the infraction as a felony. By the time the papers got around to issuing corrections and retractions, the primary election was over.

Though Sarah Palin narrowly lost her bid to be the Republican nominee for lieutenant governor in 2002, Senator Frank Murkowski easily won his bid to be the nominee for governor, and then went on to defeat sitting Lieutenant Governor Fran Ulmer in the general election by the widest margin in Alaska's brief history.

It then fell to the victorious Murkowski to nominate his own replacement to serve out the balance of his six-year term in the Senate. Sarah had been told she was on Murkowski's short list of candidates for that job. Soon she was summoned to Juneau for a face-to-face interview with the incoming executive. As she relates in her autobiography, she walked away from that interview with the distinct impression that she would not be Murkowski's pick. His comments strongly indicated he felt the brutal Beltway political scene was no place for a mother with young children. She wasn't sure she disagreed. Nor was she at all sure she even wanted the job, although she was understandably honored to be considered. Nevertheless she was stunned a few weeks later to hear that Murkowski had chosen his own daughter—a mother of two young children herself—to be his replacement.

In retrospect, the flagrantly nepotistic pick reveals a certain tone-deafness about ethics and appearances that would haunt Murkowski for his entire term. There was a large repository of good will and respect for Murkowski among Alaskans, and Palin shared it. She had campaigned enthusiastically for him across the state immediately following her own primary loss. As the long-time chairman of the Senate Energy and Natural Resources Committee, Murkowski had been a consistent champion of Alaska's interests in Washington, but eyebrows rose as the new governor appointed key players from his Beltway power-circle to key positions in his Juneau administration. Some wondered if perhaps Murkowski had been a Washington insider a little too long.

One appointment popular with many Alaskans was his choice of Sarah Palin to serve on the three-member Alaska Oil and Gas Conservation Commission (AOGCC). The commission was statutorily designed to be comprised of three individuals—one geologist, one petroleum engineer, and one representative of the public at large. A holdover from the previous administration filled the geologist slot. Palin would be the public representative, would chair the group, and serve as the ethics supervisor for the commission. It was Murkowski's pick for the third slot—the one designated for a petroleum engineer—

that sent critical tongues wagging across the state. The post went to the state Republican Party chairman Randy Ruedrich.

Ruedrich was certainly qualified for the job. He had several advanced degrees in chemical engineering and had been working in the petroleum industry most of his adult life. The problem for some was that he also planned to remain in position as chairman of the state Republican Party. In fact, it had been Ruedrich who had pushed for Palin to be placed on the AOGCC. He saw her as a rising star in the party and saw himself as her principal sponsor and groomer for bigger things down the road.

He would shortly find out what Nick Carney discovered after encouraging Sarah to run for the city council—that Palin's ultimate loyalty was not to patron or to party, but to principle.

The other familiar pattern here was Sarah's energetic approach to her new position. She asked long-time commission staffers to recommend books, and she devoured reams of state regulations and records of past commission rulings. She wasn't expected to know engineering and geology. That's what the other two positions on the panel were for. But it was her way to master every challenge—and she was determined to press and grind and cram until she was confident she could pull her own weight and then some.

As it happened, her primary challenge as a commissioner came not in her role as an overseer of oil and gas production projects but as the overseer of ethics within the commission. Just months after beginning her new job, she started hearing complaints about Ruedrich doing Republican Party business on AOGCC time and using commission resources.

Palin's options for handling these complaints were tightly restricted by statute. She went through the proper channels and up the chain of command, but nothing was done. After months of fruitless attempts to get the appropriate officials in the Murkowski government to take action in what was a widening scandal, a desperately frustrated Palin decided to write a letter to Murkowski himself, even though she was convinced doing so would likely mean the end of her political aspirations. In *Going Rogue* she later wrote:

> As I typed out the words, I thought, *This is it. I'm taking on the party and putting it in writing. My career is over. Well, if I die, I die.*[8]

"If I die, I die." It is a phrase that surfaces again and again in Palin's life. Five years later in her speech resigning the governorship of Alaska, she used the same words. In both cases she was making a move that seemed to be career suicide. The words are saturated with meaning. They are, in fact, a window into Palin's values system and into her view of herself as well.

Students of the Bible will recognize this beloved phrase as coming from the Book of Esther, the biblical story of a young Jewish woman of humble background living among the exiles in Persia in the fifth century before Christ. In the narrative, Esther finds herself suddenly elevated to a place of influence—one in which she is uniquely positioned to save her people, but at the possible cost of her own life. As she wrestles with her decision, a father figure asks her to consider a possibility concerning God's providence: "Who knows but that you have come to royal position for such a time as this?"[9] Once Esther decides to risk all in order to do the right thing, she seals her resolve with a statement of abandonment to the will of God: "If I die, I die."

This same sense of abandonment filled Palin as she sent her letter. Events were in the hands of God, she believed. And as either fate or providence ordained, Palin's letter was received just as the story began to break wide open in the media. The truth began to come out, and Ruedrich was forced to resign.

Still, this didn't end Palin's problems. The media and the Democrats were demanding an investigation into what had been going on within the AOGCC. They weren't going to let Murkowski's people sweep the matter under the rug. Yet, to Palin, that seemed to be exactly what the governor's team planned to do, and it left her in an awkward, painful position.

The state's rules forbade Sarah from speaking publicly about the internal affairs of the commission, a point the state's Department of Law had emphasized by essentially issuing a gag order upon the two remaining commission members. The only person who could speak publicly and clear the air was Murkowski himself, and he was acting as if the problem didn't exist.

The Democrats and the press engaged in wild speculation, accusing Sarah of covering up a scandal. Behind the scenes, Republican heavyweights were telling her not to rock the boat, or she risked destroying her future prospects in the party. Eventually, she took the only route that offered her the freedom to speak openly about the ethical problems she'd seen. On January 16, 2004, scarcely more than one year after taking her seat on the AOGCC, she resigned.

Not long thereafter, the state's attorney general finally issued a sixteen-page ethics complaint against Ruedrich and levied the largest civil fine in Alaskan history. Sarah was seen by many as a hero in the matter, but now she was a hero without a role or the power to bring change.

Meanwhile, though few could have guessed it at the time, more scandal storms were brewing on the horizon in Juneau and Anchorage. Soon the political climate would be ripe for a reform-minded outsider with libertarian principles. To Palin, it meant that she might be the right woman at just the right time, or, in the words of her favorite story, that she might have come into perfect position "for such a time as this."

Chapter 11

FIVE SMOOTH STONES

*Leaders are visionaries with a poorly developed sense of
fear and no concept of the odds against them.*[1]
—ROBERT JARVIK

T HE TRIANGLE CLUB SITS AT THE CORNER OF FRONT STREET
and Franklin in the heart of Juneau's historic district and just
three and a half short blocks from the state capitol building. Like
many of the structures in the old part of the city it exudes rustic
charm, but it is far from fancy. Nondescript on the outside. Dark and
smoky on the inside. In spite of this, or perhaps because of it, the
Triangle Club is a favorite meeting place for state legislators, staff
members, and lobbyists.

On the evening of March 26, 2006, a bombshell op-ed that ran
simultaneously in all three of the state's major newspapers that day
had the place buzzing. Lori Backes had penned the piece. She was
the head of the *All Alaska Alliance*, a group formed to advocate a gas
pipeline strategy that did not involve big, multinational oil corporations. The headline above the piece read "Follow the Money to
Governor's Gas Deal." In it Backes was critical of Governor Frank
Murkowski and the state legislature—specifically their approach to
rewriting the system under which oil companies would be taxed in

the future. She also decried the secretive negotiations Murkowski was conducting with three major oil companies about getting a gas pipeline built. She pointed out that oil-related companies and their executives were, by far, the biggest contributors to political campaigns in the state, but her criticisms went further.

She also reported that one particular oil field services company, the VECO Corporation, was the largest single source of contributions. There was more. She listed the names of eleven state legislators along with Governor Murkowski and itemized how much each of the twelve individuals had received in contributions from VECO-connected sources. The amounts ranged from $8,000 to $24,000. She did not assert that any of the contributions were illegal. She simply pointed out who was a significant butterer of certain key legislators' bread:

> This is not intended to pick on any particular legislator. Many Alaskans make their living off the oil industry, and many individuals and organizations donate to political campaigns. But it does show how much VECO and the producers are willing to invest in our state government. Have these financial linkages and political investments afforded "undue influence" over Alaska's political players and process? Perhaps not, but certain actions might suggest otherwise.[2]

That evening some of the legislators named in the editorial were sitting at a corner booth in the Triangle Club discussing the insinuations of Backes's piece. Suddenly, a bar patron who may have had one too many walked up to the table and yelled, "You corrupt bastards!" and then walked out the door.

The men stared at each other in stunned silence for a moment and then simultaneously broke out into uncontained laughter. The awkward moment became a bit of a running joke with the group. In future meetings at the bar they would jokingly refer to themselves as the Corrupt Bastards Club or the Corrupt Bastards Caucus. One member of the group went as far as to have golf caps made up with the initials CBC emblazoned on them.

No one was laughing five months later when the FBI raided the offices of six of the eleven legislators mentioned in Backes's editorial.

Sarah Palin is a *stickler*.

It is a term Lynne Truss uses frequently in her classic and surprisingly fun book on grammar and usage, *Eats, Shoots and Leaves: The Zero Tolerance Approach to Punctuation*. As the subtitle suggests, it refers to people like herself who carry the conviction that it is never OK to be sloppy where the written word is concerned. Regarding the manifold trials and woes of people like herself she writes:

> Part of one's despair, of course, is that the world cares nothing for the little shocks endured by the sensitive stickler. While we look in horror at a badly punctuated sign, the world carries on around us, blind to our plight. We are like the little boy in *The Sixth Sense* who can see dead people, except that we can see dead punctuation.[3]

Palin clearly has the stickler's temperament, but not in the realm of grammar and usage—as anyone who has heard her speak extemporaneously would probably suspect. She is a stickler about constitutions—state and federal. Her oft-stated conviction is that the U.S. Constitution is a brilliantly crafted document, that it means only what the craftsmen intended when they wrote it, and that it should constrain the federal government's reach with chains of steel.

This trait explains a big part of Palin's appeal within the Tea Party movement. There is a strong streak of originalist constitutionalism that runs through it, as well. Not surprisingly, she received a huge roar of approval when, as the keynote speaker at the very first Tea Party convention in Nashville on February 6, 2010, she thundered:

The problems that we face in the real world require real solutions, and we'd better get to it because the risks that they pose are great and they're grave. However, as Barry Goldwater said, we can be conquered by bombs, but we can also be conquered by neglect, by ignoring our Constitution and disregarding the principles of limited government.[4]

She was equally strong in her views about Alaska's state constitution. Her associates often reported that, first as a member of AOGCC and later as governor, Palin kept a copy of the Alaska constitution with her at all times. Occasionally, when referring to it in a discussion or a speech, she would pull it out and wave it in the air for emphasis. She frequently called it *the good book*.

In 2005, as ethical questions about Murkowski's handling of two vital and interrelated issues concerning the oil and gas industry multiplied, Palin—the freshly liberated private citizen—would have lots of opportunities to wave that document around.

Bill McAllister—the veteran print and television journalist who was among the first to reach Palin in Barrow the day three members of the Corrupt Bastards Caucus were arrested—believes that Palin has enjoyed the most extraordinary *luck* in timing of any politician he has ever observed. Later, as her director of communications during the wildest year of her governorship, he would come up with a name for this amazing knack of being in the right place at the right time with the right message. He called it *Sarah-dipity*.

Her high-profile resignation from the Alaska Oil and Gas Conservation Commission in January of 2004 had removed the legal gag from Sarah's mouth. In editorials, interviews, and speeches, she spoke out clearly but circumspectly about what had happened inside the commission in order to clear the air. She assumed that she had already burned several bridges with the operators of the state's Republican Party machinery, but there was no point in throwing gasoline on the fires or running the risk of seeming vindictive. She moved back into full-time-mom mode and concentrated on enjoying her children. She became the manager for fifteen-year-old Track's hockey team and allowed the sports reporter side of her life to emerge once more.

As 2004 unfolded, however, Palin grew increasingly alarmed about what she was seeing and hearing of Murkowski's approach to state government—leading her to the conclusion that her negative experience with the AOGCC represented a pattern of disregard for proper process and transparency. By the middle of 2005, she was giving serious thought to challenging Murkowski in the 2006 Republican primary, a move that would surely infuriate the Republican Party establishment from which she was already estranged. She was undecided, wrestling, trying to weigh her home life against her sense of political calling, the possibility of winning if she ran against the Republican backlash that would certainly ensue.

A friend's phone call that summer helped move her from ambivalence to action. Rick Halford was a former state senate president pro tempore representing the Chugiak area on the northern edge of Anchorage. He was also a family friend who had recently married a childhood acquaintance of Todd.

He was calling to deliver a message. After itemizing everything he viewed as wrongheaded about the current administration's methods and plans, he got to the point: "Sarah, I think you should run for governor." She confessed that she had been thinking about it, but then offered an itemized list of her own. She rattled off a half a dozen reasons why it would be a long shot, uphill, almost kamikaze effort to challenge a sitting Republican governor, particularly one of Murkowski's colossal stature. Halford's response surprised her.

"Sarah, you have five stones in your hand."

She instantly recognized the reference to the biblical story of David and his courageous battle with the giant Goliath. She had heard the story from the seventeenth chapter of the Book of 1 Samuel countless times. "Then [David] took his staff in his hand, chose five smooth stones from the stream, put them in the pouch of his shepherd's bag and, with his sling in his hand, approached the Philistine."[5] Is there a person in the Western world who doesn't know how that story ends?

Halford went on to elaborate on his cryptic statement. He said he believed Palin's people-of-Alaska-first positions on the key issues were the smooth stones that would make her victorious if she only summoned the courage to face the giant. As Palin later recounted in *Going Rogue*: "'You have the five stones,' Rick said in one of those calls. 'You have the right positions on ethics, on energy, on government's appropriate role. It's an out-of-the-box idea and you won't get the establishment's support, but I think you should run for governor. Our state is ready for change.'"[6]

Sarah had been praying, asking for guidance and wisdom about the run. And as every Christian who has ever wrestled with a difficult decision has done, she asked God for some kind of sign to indicate that the direction her heart seemed to be pulling was the right one. Halford's call was her sign. From that day forward, she began quietly planning her campaign. She silently and methodically gathered her smooth stones.

In this season of Palin's preparation, two issues of supreme importance to Alaskans dominated the headlines in the state papers and led the nightly news. The first involved the *production profits tax* (PPT), a complex scheme through which oil and gas production was taxed in Alaska. It was the state's primary source of revenue. There was widespread agreement that the current approach was broken. Collected revenues had been dropping year after year for some time, even in times when the oil companies' profits were high.

The second issue was a contract being negotiated by the Murkowski administration with the Big Three oil companies—one that would make the long-sought gas pipeline from the North Slope a reality.

The Big Three were ExxonMobil, ConocoPhillips, and BP (formerly British Petroleum). There were other Alaska-based companies interested in talking to the state about building a gas line too, but they had not been invited to participate in the conversation. This was the principal complaint of Lori Backes's All Alaska Alliance. Palin thought it was a mistake as well, and she said so often.

These are complex subjects, and eyes can quickly begin to glaze over when presented with the arcana and detail necessary for a full understanding. At a minimum, it is important to understand that the two issues were very much interrelated.

They were connected because it was a given that Murkowski would be offering the Big Three some combination of incentives, tax breaks, and guarantees in return for a commitment to build the pipeline. The problem was, no one knew what that combination looked like or what it would cost the state. Murkowski refused to say, claiming the negotiations were sensitive and secret. Meanwhile the legislature was being asked to rewrite the scheme under which those companies would be taxed for the indefinite future—but was being required to do so in the dark. Legislators on both sides of the aisle thought this was madness.

In an op-ed in the *Mat-Su Valley Frontiersman*, Palin urged legislators to hold off voting on the production profits tax until they had seen the gas pipeline fiscal contract. "Until we see otherwise, it appears [Murkowski is] gambling public assets and...claiming to have won the game while refusing to put all the cards on the table to prove it."[7]

On October 18, 2005, Palin made the formal announcement that she was running as a Republican for the governorship of the state of Alaska. In her announcement speech, she criticized the current administration and sounded themes of reform, high ethical standards, and transparency. Her positions were not only conservative but populist as well. She declared it was "time to take a stand and put Alaska

first." Almost immediately she experienced a huge dose of McAllister's Sarah-dipity. Less than a week after launching a reform-centric
campaign and calling for a cleanup of corruption, the Murkowski
administration found itself caught up in a huge ethical fiasco involving
the state's Department of Natural Resources (DNR).

Two days after Palin's official announcement, the head of the
DNR, Tom Irwin, sent the state's attorney general a private memo
asking some basic questions about the legality of certain aspects of the
governor's secret negotiations with the Big Three. Instead of replying,
the attorney general handed the memo over to Governor Murkowski,
who, obviously offended by the questions, made the memo public and
put Irwin on administrative leave. A few days later, Irwin was fired
amid a flurry of press attention.

Irwin was respected by Democrats and Republicans alike and
much beloved within the department. Upon his dismissal, six senior
DNR officials resigned in protest, triggering another massive wave
of media coverage around the state. Someone within the oil and
gas division of the DNR admiringly dubbed the entire group *The
Magnificent Seven*. The name stuck, and they became a symbol for
much that Alaskans considered wrong with the Murkowski government. His approval ratings plummeted.

The challenger who had just launched an anticorruption campaign
had been handed the gift of a lifetime. Sarah fired off an op-ed in
which she called Irwin and the six *a superb team* and their loss to
the state *shameful*. "They should be ushered back into state service
so we might again benefit from their expertise and integrity. I'd hire
them," she declared.[8] And indeed, when she became governor, that is
precisely what she did.

Palin's campaign quickly gained traction. Still, the reaction from
the Republican Party leadership to Palin's run was negative. At one
point in the campaign she got a call from state senator Ben Stevens,
the sitting president of the senate and son of U.S. Senator Ted

Stevens. He was furious at Palin. "You're not just running against Murkowski," he told her. "You're running against me, my dad—the whole state Republican Party."[9] And in a very real sense she was. But a lot of rank-and-file Republicans, and a lot of Independents and Democrats, felt very much as Palin did. They viewed her as a voice for their concerns and a champion of their interests.

As the campaign entered 2006, Murkowski continued his steadfast refusal to disclose details of the contract he had negotiated with the Big Three and was equally adamant that the legislature should pass the new production profits tax bill he introduced in February of that year.

The more Alaskans learned of how Murkowski was handling the negotiations on the pipeline contract, the greater their concern grew that he was giving away the store. State Representative Eric Croft, a Democrat from Anchorage who was also running for governor, said, "I think it's a sad day.... One hundred thirty-nine years ago Russia sold Alaska for peanuts, and we just sold Alaska's oil for peanuts. I think we're going to get a gut check on this legislature and finally find out who owns this state."[10]

Even those inclined to give the governor the benefit of the doubt were beginning to wonder if the years Murkowski and his team spent in Washington had made them overly empathetic to the oil companies' concerns. Those less inclined to be charitable suspected Big Oil's money had purchased the hearts and minds of the Murkowski team, along with those of more than a few legislators as well.

Palin articulated many of these concerns in a March 19, 2006, op-ed in the *Mat-Su Valley Frontiersman*. It is worth quoting at length for the insight it offers into the issues themselves and into Palin's balanced, Constitution-centered approach:

> [Oil industry] negotiators are some of the sharpest professionals on earth, with decades of experience dedicated to their

company's bottom line. Our negotiators are citizen legislators or political appointees who sometimes are dependent on the industry for their next job.

It may look like we're outgunned at the table, but thankfully we can compete because we've got supremely powerful ammunition. It's called the Alaska Constitution, and it provides our strength as we deal with corporations whose ultimate goal is to make themselves maximum profit and leave as little as possible behind.

I respect industry's contributions to our economy as it pumps our oil, gets it to market, and makes mind-boggling profit off our resources. I personally appreciate the blue-collar job opportunities industry provides. I am, in fact, married to a Slope worker, so I'm not out to bash the industry, nor do I expect officials to use a hammer in negotiations. But I do expect us to stop acting weak and confused and just do the right thing for Alaskans, via our Constitution.

Here's what the Constitution says: Negotiate for the maximum benefit of all Alaskans. Period. That must be the objective. It really is that straightforward.[11]

Clearly, Palin believed, as did an overwhelming majority of Alaskans, that since 99 percent of all Alaska lands are locked up by the state and federal government, leaving little for private ownership, that all citizens of Alaska should benefit from the natural resource wealth those lands contain.

As her campaign rolled toward a primary showdown with Murkowski, events continued to work in Palin's favor. On May 5, a judge ordered Governor Murkowski to reveal the details of the contract he had negotiated with the Big Three. Murkowski did not comply immediately, and the next day Palin addressed a large crowd that had gathered outside the state capitol complex to protest Murkowski's secrecy. Her populist message was gaining her support, while Murkowski's missteps only increased. Moved by either spite or desperation, Murkowski waited until May 10, the day *after* the legislative session ended, to comply with the judge's order. It had all become too much. Murkowski's popularity plummeted. On August 22, Republican voters went to the polls to choose their preferred candidate for governor. Palin won handily. A humiliated Murkowski finished third.

Palin's work was only half done. She would be facing a formidable opponent in the general election. The Democratic primary had been won by former two-term governor Tony Knowles. Still, Sarah-dipity reigned. One week after the primary election, FBI agents raided the offices of six state legislators, all members of the self-described Corrupt Bastards Caucus. The shocking headlines further confirmed the validity of Palin's campaign themes. Her popularity skyrocketed, and Tony Knowles could not keep pace. When the votes were counted on November 4, Sarah Palin was the clear winner.

The oil and gas industry recognized it was a new day in Alaska politics. As Bill McAllister has said:

> You have to understand [Alaska's] background to appreciate how huge what Palin did really was. She campaigned on, and delivered on the idea of saying to these Big Three oil companies, "No. We're not going to negotiate with you alone and lock all other interested parties out of the process. We're going to publicly announce what the people of the state of Alaska need for this to be a win for them, and then we're going to see who wants to give it to them." She completely scrambled the game. It's one of the major events since statehood.[12]

One anonymous industry insider speaking to a reporter for the *Petroleum News* summed it up this way: "Now they've got Sarah Palin. And they're in for the surprise of their lives."[13]

The oil and gas executives weren't the only ones to be startled by the unorthodox young woman who was now sitting behind the chief executive's desk. Long-time politicos were shocked, and working

Alaskans were delighted to see the new governor immediately start delivering on her campaign promise to run the state government like a frugal homemaker on a tight budget.

One of her first acts was to reassign the full-time chef on staff at the governor's mansion. She felt awkward about asking a trained chef to cater to her family's simple tastes and felt it unseemly to be waited on. She feared the impact it would have on the souls of her younger children. "I don't want them thinking when I'm done being governor that it's normal to have a chef. It's OK for them to have macaroni and cheese." For his part, Todd set about identifying various leaky spots in the roof of the old place and overseeing repairs. The Palins insisted on doing the First Family role in their own unique way.

As a candidate, Palin had been critical of Murkowski's purchase of a corporate jet with state money and without legislative approval. Shortly after Palin took office, the $2.7 million Westwind II jet went up for sale on eBay, as promised. The listing featured a picture of a man standing beside the aircraft holding a sign. It read, "For Sale By Owner: The People of Alaska." The eBay listing was less a primary strategy for liquidating the plane and more just a dramatic way to make a point. No bids were received, but the jet finally sold a few months later through a traditional broker. Meanwhile Palin traveled as much or more than Murkowski but at a fraction of the cost to the state. In addition to its hefty price tag, the Westwind II cost roughly $1,700 per hour to fly. Palin took commuter flights on Alaska Airlines when possible and borrowed a King Air turboprop airplane from the Department of Public Safety the rest of the time.

The travel budget for the governor's office dropped from $520,000 in Murkowski's final year to $114,000 in Palin's first. The last time Murkowski attended the National Governors' Conference in Washington DC, he stayed at a $937 per night suite at the JW Marriott and ran up a bill that cost the state $6,600. A year later when Palin attended, she chose a hotel at less than half the rate with a total cost of $1,885.[14]

She was resolute in fulfilling her campaign promises. She played hardball with the big oil companies, began rebuilding bridges of trust and communication between the governor's office and the legislature, worked to minimize the tax burden on Alaskans and to maximize the payouts from the Permanent Fund. Before her first term was up, Palin's popularity rating had risen to a jaw-dropping 93 percent.[15] She was, simply stated, the most popular Republican politician in the nation.

Her rise had not been meteoric. There had been more rapid ascents in American political life. Still, her story was astonishing. It had been as recently as 1992 when Palin had never held political office, nurtured only a faint hope of fulfilling her childhood dream of public service, and was likely to be an oil-field worker's wife for the rest of her life. Then came the city council and the mayor's office and her rise to governor, all in barely a dozen years. What made it all so stunning was that Palin was never the smartest, best-funded, or most experienced candidate in her races. Nor was she the most articulate or the best connected to sources of power. Instead, she had risen through character, by winning respect from voters through openness and truth. It sounds hackneyed in the retelling, and it has caused more than one Washington DC pundit to scoff, but there is little doubt that what fueled Sarah Palin's political rise were the values and moral principles she had learned from family and church, and which she then had the courage to apply to her political roles. This is what won her honor in Alaska. This is what brought her to national attention. And this is what eventually moved John McCain to try to merge the Sarah Palin story with his own.

Section 2 Afterword

SIX PILLARS OF SARAH PALIN'S POLITICS

I T WOULD BE EASY TO LIST SARAH PALIN'S CORE POLITICAL principles. She has expounded these with clarity, and they are widely shared. Even the most casual observer knows that she is in favor of a constitutionally limited federal government, low taxes, strong defense, protection of the unborn, decentralized political authority, and the primacy of private property and the free market. There is no secret here, nothing new to explore.

What is less known are the principles by which she has conducted herself in politics. These have defined her life of public leadership and will continue to do so in the years to come. They are the more critical factors in what she will do with the public position she has acquired and what type of impact she will have on American society. They are also critical to understanding what might be called the *Palin style of leadership*.

1. Those unwilling to surrender power are not worthy to have power.

At two critical junctures in Sarah Palin's life she has surrendered power when she thought it served the broader good. When she could not end the corruption on the Alaska Oil and Gas Conservation Commission, she resigned in order to tell the people the truth. When she returned to Alaska from her vice-presidential campaign and found herself besieged by lawsuits and ethics probes, she resigned as governor so the business of the state could be done. This has evolved into a principle of her life. Those who grasp power are unworthy of it and should be suspect, but those willing to give power up for the good of those they serve are worthy of greater power still.

2. The measure of good government is the good of the people.

Throughout her political life, Palin has kept her eye on the good of the people. When she opposed big oil in Alaska, it was because the people were ill served. When she fought a measure in Wasilla on a matter as small as garbage collection, she did it, again, because she believed the lives of people would not have been improved unless she did. This is the focus of her populist conservatism, and it has become the yardstick by which she measures all government actions. Do the people benefit? Are their freedoms increased? Will a law or a service benefit both the people living today and their children's children? This is the measure of political action for Sarah Palin, and it is a counter to the self-serving strain in public service today.

3. Constitutions are covenants between the government and the governed. Without them there is no legitimate political power.

It must have been entertaining to see Governor Sarah Palin pull a copy of the Alaska constitution out of her pocket or her purse, hold it aloft, and call it *the good book*. It was good political theater. But Palin was trying to make a larger point. Constitutions are covenants, contracts between the people and their government. Elected leaders are bound by these covenants and cannot stray from the roles they prescribe. Without them you have only monarchs exercising authority as they choose. For Palin, nothing could be more repugnant to a nation of laws and to the constitutional boundaries that preserved freedom and order through the years.

4. Private industry is of value, but private industry tethered to government is fascism.

Sarah Palin is a free market, private property, pro-business conservative. Yet she has seen the corruption that comes from government yielded to corporate power, to government as an extension of business rather than as a check on business. It is what Mussolini attempted in Italy during World War II, and it is what Americans opposed as at odds with freedom and democratic ways. This is what distinguishes Palin from many of the conservatives on the national scene today. She is suspicious of Wall Street and of the influence of lobbyists and money in government. This is what has set her at the head of the Tea Party movement and as the voice of popular backlash to the bailouts and public ownership of industries that have become common today.

5. Public service is a privilege to be honored, not a luxury to be enjoyed.

Sarah Palin became the most popular Republican politician in the nation in 2008 largely because she rejected the corrupt, privileged culture of the Frank Murkowski administration. She sold the famous private jet and flew commercial airlines. She traveled as though the money she spent wasn't hers. It wasn't. She also fired the chef in the governor's mansion, cut household staff, and even reduced her own security to bring spending into line. This had huge popular appeal, but it was also in keeping with Palin's philosophy. Elected leaders are not potentates; they are servants. They should enjoy public service but never forget that the benefits of their service accrue to the people, not to themselves.

6. Tell the people the truth, and justice will result.

It is intriguing that while Palin is not the most articulate politician in America, she is skilled at getting her meaning across. No one leaves her speeches wondering what she believes. She is committed to the idea that telling the people the truth is the key to justice being done. This is why she resigned the Alaska Oil and Gas Conservation Commission. As long as she was on the commission, she could not speak to the people. Once she could, the people heard her words and demanded justice be done. Palin is no high-flying orator, but she is devoted to telling the truth and letting the people decide.

Section 3

THE NATIONAL STAGE

Chapter 12

MCCAIN

In forty hours I shall be in battle, with little information, and on the spur of the moment will have to make the most momentous decisions. But I believe that one's spirit enlarges with responsibility and that, with God's help, I shall make them, and make them right.

—GENERAL GEORGE S. PATTON

IT WAS AUGUST 29, 2008, AND BOB HECKMAN, A MEMBER OF John McCain's senior strategic team responsible for conservative and religious voters, was eagerly scanning the staff room television at McCain's campaign headquarters in hopes of discovering who the candidate's vice-presidential pick would be. It was tense, and the recent rumors had not helped. Members of Mitt Romney's staff and family had been telling reporters for weeks that he was McCain's choice. Now, though, as the hour of the announcement neared in Dayton, Ohio, Romney was nowhere to be found. Governor Tim Pawlenty of Minnesota was also a much-discussed possibility, but there had already been a Pawlenty sighting elsewhere that morning. His selection seemed unlikely. Someone had even mentioned a single wire story about a plane coming in from Alaska, but given the events of the day, it seemed too insignificant to matter.

Heckman kept his eyes on the television set but got on the

phone with a fellow staffer who was helping him prepare for that afternoon's meeting with the Council for National Policy (CNP). Founded by evangelical leader Tim LaHaye and comprised of many of the country's leading social conservatives, the CNP meeting was an important one, and Heckman wanted to make sure all the details were right. The man Heckman was speaking to was on a pay phone two blocks away from where McCain was about to announce his vice-presidential choice.

Then it happened. McCain was suddenly at the podium quieting the screaming crowd and beginning his remarks. He had found the *right partner* he said, someone who had "stood up to special interests," who had "stopped government from wasting taxpayers' money," and who had "put it back to work for the people." This person had "executive experience," had worked on the problem of foreign oil dependency, and was a union member married to a union member. McCain said his choice had been a high school point guard, a PTA member, a mayor, a governor, and a person of the highest integrity.

Heckman's mind reeled. Who was it? The choice had been a closely guarded secret within the campaign. In fact, it had been one of the best-protected secrets that he had seen in his nearly three decades in politics. He was sure that barely half a dozen people knew whom McCain had chosen.

Then Heckman, still on the phone, heard McCain say that his choice was "a devoted wife and mother of five."

"My God," Heckman thought, "it's Palin."

And then, in a few moments, McCain announced: "My friends and fellow Americans, I am very pleased and very privileged to introduce to you the next vice president of the United States—Governor Sarah Palin of the great state of Alaska."

The crowd erupted. Heckman could hear the roar of approval through the phone. In the staff room where he stood, people wept. "It was just the power of the moment," Heckman later said. "They wept because she was a woman. They wept because she represented what many of us in the campaign cared about: America. Traditions. Roots. They wept because the choice of Palin meant there was a chance for victory."

Heckman knew that Palin's selection would likely mean great gains among the religious and conservative voters it was his job to reach. Just how much difference Palin made became obvious that afternoon at the CNP meeting. After preliminaries, the moment came for Focus on the Family's founder, Dr. James Dobson, to speak. Dobson was nearly the social conservatives' pope, and Heckman hoped for his blessing on the Palin decision. With Dobson, though, you could never be sure. The aging psychologist had been difficult and confusing during this election. Early on he had attacked McCain for everything from failing to support a constitutional amendment protecting marriage to having a bad temper and using foul language. Later, Dobson had viciously attacked Fred Thompson, questioning not only Thompson's commitment to social conservatism but even whether Thompson was a Christian as he claimed. Then, as oddly, Dobson finally endorsed Arkansas Governor Mike Huckabee just weeks before Huckabee was forced to drop out of the presidential race, but far too late to do the candidate any good.

Heckman hoped for better this time. He soon got it. Once Dobson took the podium to address the CNP at the Dayton Hilton that afternoon, he immediately began heaping praise on Palin. She was the right choice, Dobson insisted, a choice that could turn the election. "He showered praise," Heckman recalled later. "The crowd rose to its feet in approval, and I knew we had a hit."

McCain knew it too. Not long afterward, Heckman saw McCain at a campaign stop. During the usual meet and greet McCain turned to Heckman and said, "I did good, didn't I, Bobby?" referring to the Palin decision.

"Yes, sir," Heckman assured. "You did good."

McCain, beaming, repeated gleefully, "I sure did," before turning to shake still more hands.[1]

McCain had indeed chosen well. He had been fully five points down in the polls as Barack Obama emerged from one of the most successful Democratic Conventions in history. McCain knew he had to do something huge, something dramatic, something that would rescue him even from the uninspiring tone of his own campaigning.

Yet the process that led to the Palin decision said much about what was wrong with the McCain campaign in the eyes of many Republicans and also about why hopes for a Palin rescue were so high.

It is telling that the man John McCain most wanted for his vice president was Connecticut senator Joe Lieberman. The two men liked each other, enjoyed time together, and respected each other's character. The warrior in McCain also liked that Lieberman had once fought back against the power brokers in his own Democratic Party, had resigned, run as an Independent, and won. Lieberman liked that McCain was a true political maverick who, like himself, often defied conservative/liberal categories. It also touched McCain that Lieberman had risked his own political career to join the Straight Talk Express and openly campaign for a Republican. Loyalty went a long way with John McCain.

Still, there was no getting around the fact that Lieberman was liberal on every major issue except national security. His pro-abortion views alone were enough to scuttle the ticket, and aides warned that if McCain chose Lieberman, he risked a convention walkout of social conservatives. With a split party and no support from the religious base, there could be no victory.

Typically, McCain fumed and argued. In time he came to see that it could not be Lieberman. Mitt Romney was considered and much debated, but advisors like Senator Lindsey Graham assured McCain that he could never rise above the *Mormon thing*. Governor Tim Pawlenty was an option, but, as a majority of advisors insisted, "no one knows who he is, and the snore factor is huge." No, Pawlenty was a nice guy, but he would do nothing to ignite the campaign. Tom Ridge, governor of Pennsylvania, was also pondered briefly, but, again, he was pro-choice, and McCain's team believed a pro-abortion vice president would mean certain defeat.

A few other options were thrown about, but none captured the imagination. Then Sarah Palin was mentioned again. She had been on some of the lists for consideration, but with heavyweights like Lieberman and Romney to consider, Palin never came up for serious discussion.

"I'll call her," McCain decided after brief discussion.

The decision to go with Sarah Palin for vice president was among the most personal of McCain's career. He was a true maverick who often went with feel over philosophy, and this was the most important decision of his political life. He wanted to meet Palin, get a sense of her. He would leave the vetting to others, but ultimately he would make the call, and he would do so on the basis of what he believed after taking stock of the young Alaska governor.

On August 27 Palin flew from Anchorage to Flagstaff, Arizona, to begin the process. After lengthy and detailed meetings with McCain aides, she was driven to the candidate's ranch to meet with the senator and his wife. Palin was hard not to like. She was pretty, intelligent, and fun. She was also, according to the polls, the most popular Republican politician in the nation, and she was a conservative's conservative. John and Cindy McCain liked her immediately.

There were more meetings with the candidate and more late-night vetting sessions by McCain senior staff. Finally, a senior advisor put it to McCain straight: "John, high risk, high reward."

McCain didn't hesitate. "You shouldn't have told me that. I've been a risk taker all of my life."

Palin was in.

She would do much good for the campaign, and certainly chief among her gifts was her winning way with the religious base of the Republican Party. She was a true believer, a rare politician who was religiously outspoken without being hokey, who could mention God and her religious vision without seeming to wrap herself hypocritically in insincere religious garb. Her politics, her personal life, and her faith seemed to be part of the same seamless garment. The religious Right saw her as one of their own and welcomed her.

Palin mastered an integration of faith into politics that McCain never seemed able to achieve. Indeed, already his campaign had endured one misstep of faith after another, and it had cost him dearly. Early on, McCain, knowing he needed help with the party's religious base, began courting favor with prominent evangelicals. He first went after eminent televangelist Rod Parsley, who had worked so effectively for George W. Bush's win in Ohio. McCain courted Parsley, but the internationally revered pastor was cautious. He knew of McCain's hesitations about abortion, knew that he had not supported a defense of marriage amendment to the Constitution, and was in favor of stem cell research. Then there was the reputation for raging and vile language. Still, Parsley was an astute student of American politics, and he recognized how narrow a religious conservative's options were in the present election. He decided to endorse McCain. Yet nearly as soon as he did, some impolitic statements about Islam were lifted from Parsley's *New York Times* best-selling book *Culturally Incorrect*. Reporters began branding Parsley as McCain's Jeremiah Wright—a reference to Barack Obama's problems with his outspoken pastor of many years—and McCain responded by rejecting Parsley's endorsement and denouncing the pastor's statements on Islam, leaving Parsley dazed and humiliated.

Desperate for the imprimatur of the religious Right, the McCain team then began courting the endorsement of fiery Pentecostal pastor John Hagee, founder of a San Antonio megachurch. Like Parsley, Hagee understood the field and agreed to endorse McCain. Yet when stridently anti-Catholic statements from Hagee's sermons were circulated publicly, McCain again renounced the endorsement he had worked so hard to win. It was an embarrassing second misfire, and now he was losing ground with the very religious Right he hoped to harness to his cause. Even a casual meeting with the aged Billy Graham was botched. Because of the revered evangelist's declining health, a meeting with McCain was rescheduled several times. So damaged was McCain's reputation among conservative religious leaders that rumors soon circulated that Graham had refused to meet with McCain. It wasn't true, but if it had been, few would have been surprised.

The tragedy was that McCain had a vital Christian faith of his own but, typical of many in his generation, was nearly incapable of articulating it. His father had been a high-ranking naval officer who prayed every day on his knees, Episcopal prayer book in hand. Though McCain himself was ever the nonconformist—his high school nickname was *Punk*, confirming his reputation for a "defiant, unruly streak"—he was also an altar boy who learned the confessions of Christendom—the Apostles' Creed, the Lord's Prayer—at a young age. These would serve him well years later when as a naval aviator he was shot down over North Vietnam and held as a prisoner of war for more than five hellish years. His faith sustained him, and he "prayed more often and more fervently than I ever had as a free man."[2] Because he had memorized so much of the Christian liturgies, his senior officers appointed him the chaplain to fellow POWs, and this too deepened his spiritual life. Indeed, there were worship services, particularly at Christmastime, that were "more sacred to me than any service I had attended in the past, or any service I have attended since," McCain would recall.[3]

He was released in 1973, but his life upon return spun out of control. He lost his moral bearings, and then his marriage. Despite his return to flying and then a successful run for Congress, he was spiritually at sea. He did not recover himself until he met Cindy. She was a devoted Christian who helped him reconnect to God and to his better self.

He would always look upon his years in the POW camp as his time of spiritual turning and his greatest evidence of the grace of God. There was that time on Christmas Day, for example, when a prison guard traced a cross in the sand with his foot, paused for a moment, and then walked away. God was speaking, McCain believed, and it gave him comfort. Years later, as he told this and similar stories on the campaign trail, McCain often choked up and could not continue for the tears. "I can't tell those stories anymore," McCain explained to Bob Heckman. "They mean more to me and get tougher to tell as the years go by."[4]

Somehow, though, this tenderness and faith did not translate on the campaign trail. People who searched earnestly for signs of a transforming Christianity in McCain's life often gave up disillusioned. He was hard to define. He attended North Phoenix Baptist Church with his wife, but he refused to become a member, and he refused to be baptized. He spoke of being born again in the televised forum with Pastor Rick Warren and yet did not seem to get along with any national evangelical leader. He seemed to believe in God and his goodness but could not speak about his religious life in any meaningful terms when he was *off-script*.

Then there was the issue of culture. McCain had lived his whole life around a tough, manly, violent, often-inconsistent brand of Christianity. His father prayed on his knees but regularly drank to excess. He knew military chaplains who prayed tender prayers for their men before battle, but then cussed like the damned. McCain would have had no problem calling a comrade who drank, swore, and spoke eagerly of spilling blood a *man of faith.*

This rough-hewn version of religion spilled over into his presidential campaign. McCain wrote passionately about the "faith of our fathers" and frequently reminded the country of a "divine duty." Yet so vile were the language and humor that permeated the campaign that when Sarah Palin joined the ticket, she feared for what the crassness might do to her daughters. She had never met Christians who conducted themselves in such a way. It was the difference between McCain's type of Episcopal life and Palin's Assembly of God background, between the naval base and Wasilla, Alaska. It was also the difference between winning the religious voter and losing him.

What Sarah Palin brought to the McCain campaign religiously was not only a consistency of faith and deed but also an integration of faith into public policy. She was believable not because she was well rehearsed, but rather because she had lived her faith both as personal religion and political vision. This won the religious Right by articulating what McCain could only describe haltingly, clumsily.

"She was amazing," remembers Bob Heckman. "She performed so well, articulating faith, tradition, and American values in a warm, homey manner that if it had not been for the economic meltdown of a month later, we would have won that election."[5]

Chapter 13

PROFILE: FAITH AND THE ELECTION OF 2008

This is quite a game, politics.... There are no permanent enemies, and no permanent friends. Only permanent interests.[1]

—WILLIAM CLAY

THE TRUMPET SOUNDED, AND WHEN IT DID, FEW UNDERSTOOD its meaning. Those who heard it and knew its import were among that army of the faithful ready to rise up and refashion religion in American politics from the pattern of decades. They had been waiting, and now their moment had come.

That moment was signaled at the Democratic National Convention of 2004. John Kerry, the party's nominee for president, had asked a young state senator from Illinois named Barack Obama to address the convention. Kerry had sensed something special about this intelligent, ambitious black man and wanted his story merged into the meta-narrative of his party's convention in Boston.

When Obama's speech came, all knew it was the best of the convention, perhaps one of the best in American political convention history. Obama's own symbolic journey was portrayed, of course, but there was also the call for a nobler brand of politics, a less strife-torn nation, and a more unified American life.

Then, in a sweeping passage designed to show the folly of dividing the nation into blue states (or those that tend to vote Democratic) and red states (or those that lean conservative and Republican), Obama exulted, "We worship an awesome God in the blue states."[2]

The words were a carefully crafted affirmation that religion was alive and well on the left end of the American political spectrum. *We are not all atheists*, Obama was posturing. He wanted it known that his vision—the Democrats' vision for America—was also faith-based and no less devoted than the vision of the Right. *We simply draw a different social meaning from our faith than those on the Right*, he was saying. *Our politics are also pursued in the service of God. And what is more, our time has come.*

Obama's nine words—"We worship an awesome God in the blue states"—were a signal of what was about to unfold. Between the issuing of this affirmation at the Democratic Convention in 2004 and the conclusion of the presidential election of 2008, a revolution would take place. Obama sensed it, helped to create it, and hoped to lead it. When it occurred, it would help to propel him to the presidency, but it would also leave Sarah Palin as the standard bearer for the more traditional religious consensus, and this would become the force behind much of her impact on American culture.

What Obama and his followers from the religious Left hoped to replace was a faith-based political movement that had shaped American public life for nearly three decades. It was usually referred to as the *religious Right*, and it had arisen in the mid-1970s just as the nation was approaching her bicentennial. A born-again president, Jimmy Carter, occupied the White House, and millions of religiously conservative Americans had come to believe that the country was on a course far removed from the vision of the Founding Fathers, and even further removed from the will of God. They believed the time had come for a grand restoration.

The two-hundredth anniversary of the nation's birth had forced the faith that undergirded the country's founding to the fore, and many Americans began to realize that theirs was not the secular country described in public school textbooks. Hadn't the Pilgrims sailed, as they said in their *Mayflower Compact*, "for the glory of God and the advancement of the Christian faith"? Hadn't the first Congress declared, "Religion, morality, and knowledge, being necessary to good government and the happiness of mankind, schools and the means of education shall forever be encouraged"? Weren't the speeches of nearly all the presidents filled with Bible verses and references to faith? And hadn't a justice on the U.S. Supreme Court written as late as the 1950s, "We are a religious people whose institutions presuppose a Supreme Being"?[3] This did not sound like the basis for a secular state of the kind many were then urging.

Indeed, there seemed to be a coordinated effort to remove the very foundations of faith that millions of religious Americans held dear. In 1947 the Supreme Court had ruled in *Everson v. Board of Education* that the meaning of the religious clauses of the First Amendment was a wide "separation between church and state."[4] The ruling was a break from legal tradition and a break from history— Thomas Jefferson had not penned the words "separation between church and state" until nearly a decade after the First Amendment was written, but it nevertheless became a basis for stripping the vestiges of America's religious history first from the public schools and ultimately from American public life.

There followed the largely anti-Christian cultural revolution of the 1960s, and then the Supreme Court's legalization of abortion in its 1973 *Roe v. Wade* decision. This just three years before the nation's bicentennial—and millions of religious, patriotic Americans were already convinced of the need for change.

This mood soon became a movement. In 1979, Dr. Jerry Falwell, a Baptist minister from Lynchburg, Virginia, founded the Moral Majority, which was intended to rally concerned Americans against abortion, the spread of homosexuality, antifamily laws and entertainment, and strategic concessions to the Soviet Union. The very next year, a Washington for Jesus event was attended by nearly three-quarters of a million people, according to park police, signaling a level of devotion and energy that stunned the movement's critics. At its height, the Moral Majority could boast nearly four million members and significant political influence in every state in the union.

Other combatants soon joined Falwell on the field. Dr. D. James Kennedy, pastor of the nationally influential Coral Ridge Presbyterian Church, taught widely on the faith of America's founders and on the need to return the human heart and the nation as a whole to the God of Scripture. Pat Robertson echoed this vision on his successful television network and at the university he founded to perpetuate an *American reformation*. Evangelist James Robison not only preached to packed stadiums of the need for return to the nation's God but also influenced Ronald Reagan in his decision to seek the presidency. During the Reagan years, all of these men were welcomed in the White House, and all—with many other scholars, authors, filmmakers, and pastors besides—believed that an American Christian counterrevolution was underway.

Though this rising religious Right was well funded, made ingenious use of media, mastered the new art of direct mail, and built effective coalitions that befuddled its opponents, it was the understanding of the relationship between religion and politics that was its most potent force. For men like Falwell, Robertson, and Kennedy, the Bible described more than a personal faith. It also contained a blueprint for society. In its commandments to Israel, the Scriptures gave laws that governed public morality, the conduct of courts, the function of a family, and even care for the poor. And these laws were not limited to an Old Testament people alone. In the New Testament affirmation that all "governing authorities" have been established by God, are to be considered servants of God, and derive their authority from God, many in the religious Right saw a mandate for drawing Old Testament law through the New Testament and into modern life.

This produced a brand of politics that was decidedly conservative. The religious Right of the 1980s and the 1990s fought fiercely against abortion and homosexual incursions into society; called for an educational free market to break up the monopoly of failing public schools; lobbied for limited government, low taxes, and original intent in Constitutional interpretation; and supported the strong defense posture of the Reagan and Bush years. The movement was phenomenally successful. Political campaigns were forced to address its concerns, and national debates on nearly every topic were conditioned by its priorities.

The movement's high-water mark was the 2004 reelection of George W. Bush. Though his father had been hesitant and inarticulate in matters of faith, the younger Bush was not. He had been a hard-drinking, hard-swearing, religiously indifferent man until a progression of influences landed him on a Maine beach with Billy Graham. "Reverend Graham planted a mustard seed in my soul," Bush later wrote of those few days, "a seed that grew over the next year. I had always been a religious person, had regularly attended church, even taught Sunday school and served as an altar boy. But that weekend my faith took on new meaning. It was the beginning of a new walk where I would recommit my heart to Jesus Christ. I was humbled to learn that God sent His Son to die for a sinner like me."[5]

Guided by his newfound faith, in his first term as president Bush pioneered the faith-based politics of the religious Right's dreams. He founded an Office of Faith-Based Initiatives to partner with religious institutions in doing social good. He was opposed to abortion, the homosexual community's political agenda, and embryonic stem cell research, and he made his case for all from Scripture and his understanding of God's will. He welcomed conservative religious leaders into the White House and was known to have regular communications with men like James Robison and Ted Haggard, the president of the National Association of Evangelicals (NAE). His speeches were often as theological as they were political. Typically, at his National Cathedral speech just days after the horrors of September 11, 2001, he said, "This world He [God] created is of moral design. Grief and tragedy and hatred are only for a time. Goodness, remembrance, and love have no end. And the Lord of life holds all who die and all who mourn."[6]

In the 2004 presidential race Bush was perceived as a man of faith running against a typical religious liberal with no convictions of faith to speak of. Though his Democratic opponent, John Kerry, was a committed Roman Catholic, Kerry's pro-abortion politics had caused even bishops in his own church to threaten refusing him Communion. Bush seemed the unswerving evangelical to Kerry's *flip-flopping*, hesitating liberal, the biblical man of God to the cool modernist with no transforming inner fire. Bush won, won handily, and polls revealed that faith had played a role in how some Americans voted. Bush had won the presidency again as the champion of the religious Right.

This was November of 2004. And then it all came unraveled. What followed was nearly the perfect storm of movement implosion, and the effects on the 2008 presidential election are difficult to exaggerate.

Within a year of George W. Bush's reelection, Pat Robertson, once the leading voice of the religious Right, suggested on international television that the United States would be justified in assassinating Venezuelan dictator Hugo Chávez. A few months later, Robertson asserted that Israel's prime minister, Ariel Sharon, lay in a coma because God was angry over Israeli "land for peace" policies.

The widespread scorn heaped upon Robertson in the wake of these comments compromised him in the popular mind and thus removed him from any meaningful leadership role in American politics.

Less than a year after Robertson's comments on Sharon, Ted Haggard fell into disrepute in a scandal involving drugs and homosexuality. The megachurch pastor and president of the National Association of Evangelicals had once boasted of near daily contact with the White House. Now, removed from leadership of both his Colorado Springs church and the NAE, he became a symbol of religious corruption, used by critics to attack the Bush administration's faith-based approach to governing.

This was in November of 2006. On May 15 of the next year, the world learned that Jerry Falwell, lion of the religious Right, had been found dead on his office floor. Less than six months later, Dr. D. James Kennedy was also dead. The fathers were passing from the scene, but no sons seemed destined to take their place. There simply were no prominent men of faith calling the nation to its God as Falwell, Kennedy, and Robertson had done. Those visible pastors who remained, men like T. D. Jakes, Joel Osteen, Rick Warren, and Bill Hybels, were either eager to appear nonpolitical or went to great lengths to show that they were sensitive to and in some cases sympathetic with the priorities of the political Left.

As the 2008 election approached, the fraying of the religious Right was evident. There was no galvanizing vision, no unbreakable unity, no single mighty voice with which to speak to the nation. It was confusing and, for many of the faithful, embarrassing. Pat Robertson, long a fierce anti-abortion warrior, stunned his followers when he endorsed the only pro-abortion Republican in the presidential race, Rudy Giuliani. Bob Jones III, leader of the stridently fundamentalist Bob Jones University, threw his support behind the only Mormon candidate in the race, Mitt Romney. James Dobson, as we have seen, attacked John McCain and Fred Thompson with astonishing venom early on, and then endorsed Mike Huckabee just days before Huck-abee's campaign sputtered to an end. Journalists began wondering aloud whether the current election would signal the end of the religious Right no matter who won the White House.

It did not help that the outgoing president seemed to undermine some of the basics of evangelical faith in what were called his *exit interviews*. In a televised conversation with Cynthia McFadden of ABC's *Nightline* late in December of 2008, Bush confidently explained that he is "not a literalist" in his reading of the Bible, that he does believe the God he prays to is the same as the God of the non-Christian religions, and that he believes his faith is "compatible with the scientific proof that there is evolution."[7] Evangelicals bemoaned what they viewed as the president's lack of theological awareness, and some members of the religious Left pointed out that Bush's views seemed similar to those of the incoming president, Barack Obama.

As though anticipating this dramatic ruin of the religious Right, Obama had already been calling for the American political Left to open its doors to people of faith. In a 2006 speech, given just as the religious Right was beginning to self-destruct, Obama warned that if progressives "don't reach out to evangelical Christians and other religious Americans and tell them what we stand for, then the Jerry Falwells and Pat Robertsons and Alan Keyeses will continue to hold sway."[8] Obama knew that a transitional moment had come, but it would unfold only if some treasured beliefs of the Right were challenged: "Whatever we once were, we are no longer just a Christian nation; we are also a Jewish nation, a Muslim nation, a Buddhist nation, a Hindu nation, and a nation of nonbelievers."[9]

Then came the paragraph designed to drive the dagger into the heart of the religious Right's core theology—the belief that Scripture gives laws for the governing of society.

> And even if we did have only Christians in our midst, if we expelled every non-Christian from the United States of America,

whose Christianity would we teach in the schools? Would we go with James Dobson's, or Al Sharpton's? Which passages of Scripture should guide our public policy? Should we go with Leviticus, which suggests slavery is okay and that eating shellfish is abomination? How about Deuteronomy, which suggests stoning your child if he strays from the faith? Or should we just stick to the Sermon on the Mount—a passage that is so radical that it's doubtful that our own Defense Department would survive its application? So, before we get carried away, let's read our Bibles. Folks haven't been reading their Bibles.[10]

By the campaign of 2008, the Obama team knew that many religious voters were disaffected with the political Right, and so tried to offer a new home. Obama appeared in faith forums, held closed-door meetings with evangelical leaders, and preached in churches. The campaign launched a young voter movement called the *Joshua Generation*—a name taken directly from the youth ministries of evangelical churches—led by a black Pentecostal, Joshua DuBois, which tried to win the socially conscientious, religiously active but nontraditional millennial voter.

In February of 2008, pollster and cultural analyst George Barna reported, "If the election were held today, most born-again voters would select the Democratic Party nominee for president."[11] It was a stunning turn of events. However, much to the gratitude of conservatives, a majority of born-again voters did not vote as Barna had indicated. Still, faith played a huge role in the election. Obama pulled a large percentage of evangelicals into his camp, and a massive realignment of religion in American politics was underway.

Surprisingly, it fell to Sarah Palin to champion the beliefs of the religious Right. Dobson and Robertson were compromised. Haggard had fallen from grace. Falwell and Kennedy were dead. Few other national figures were willing to articulate the political implications of a conservative brand of faith. Palin stepped happily into the fray. She had been an evangelical—indeed, a Pentecostal—since her teen years, and she did not shrink from the price of publicly proclaiming her faith. She believed in a God who ruled both heart and nation, both private and public life. She understood public policy as an outgrowth of religious worldview, and so she was, without hesitation, pro-life, pro-family, pro-faith, and for the constitutionally limited, low-tax, decentralized, strong defense version of American government that the religious Right had long portrayed as an organic outgrowth of biblical values.

After the 2008 election, the Pew Forum would report that 30 percent of news stories and a huge portion of national attention had been focused on the question of whether Barack Obama was a Muslim.[12] He wasn't, and attention to the matter was misguided. The grander religious issue playing itself out during 2008 was the dissolution of the faith-based political vision that had shaped American politics for decades and its replacement by a faith-based religious Left with Barack Obama as its leader.

The other grand theme was this: when the dust of the election settled, Sarah Palin was arguably the most visible, passionate, and articulate evangelical in American politics.

Chapter 14

GOING ROGUE?

Blessed are you when people insult you, persecute you and falsely say all kinds of evil against you because of me.... You are the light of the world. A city on a hill cannot be hidden.[1]

—JESUS OF NAZARETH

WHEN SARAH PALIN ACCEPTED JOHN MCCAIN'S INVItation to run for the vice presidency of the United States, she had already been one of the most religiously outspoken governors in the nation. Raised in a Christian home and fashioned for nearly two decades in a vibrant Assembly of God church, she had not retreated from themes of faith when she took public office.

As governor, Palin spoke openly of her Christianity and did not hesitate to mention God even in her official speeches. She was even eager to keep her ties to the church community. When a pastor she admired was celebrated in a retirement ceremony, Governor Palin dropped by the banquet unannounced and thrilled the audience by sharing how the man had changed her life. When the horrors of September 11, 2001, unfolded and prayer meetings were hosted by the larger churches in her area, she attended as many as she could. She was bold and unashamed. After attending a statewide prayer meeting in which she publicly dedicated Alaska to God, Palin later told a gathering of clergy, "And I know the Lord is not going to take it back."[2]

This was the Palin of the mayoral and gubernatorial years. She knew most Alaskans believed in God, and she knew there was no reason to hide her own devotion. She sensed that the public was weary of politicians who dithered or deflected when it came to religion, and she saw no reason to withhold. Besides, hadn't God ordained her role? Why should she dishonor Him now that He had granted her the privilege of public office?

When John McCain chose Palin as his running mate in 2008, it was in part because of this faith and the affection that it wrung from the religious base of the Republican Party. McCain had famously dynamited his relationship with these voters—courting and then criticizing famous evangelical pastors, holding views that were objectionable to the remaining vestiges of the religious Right, and having once even called Jerry Falwell and Pat Robertson "agents of intolerance" who "shame our faith, our party and our country."[3] By 2008, McCain needed help in the politics of religion, and Sarah Palin was a wise choice for this purpose.

Yet almost immediately Palin began softening her emphasis on faith. In her astonishingly successful Republican Convention speech, she referred to God only twice—once in terms of John McCain's POW experience and once to say farewell. During the campaign she claimed that she had no church affiliation, she distanced herself from her Pentecostal roots, and she was seldom specific about her religious beliefs and practices. The Republican establishment was relieved. Members of the media were confused. Evangelicals were disappointed.

There may have been good reason. From early in the campaign, Palin had not been well served in the matter of religion. The pastor at Wasilla Assembly of God, Ed Kalnins, had posted videos on the church's Web site of Palin being prayed for or Palin addressing missionary students, and these—taken out of context and with theological language unexplained—had been used as fodder by Palin's political opponents. Making matters worse, selections from Kalnins's sermons began making the rounds, further embarrassing Palin with extreme statements about critics of George W. Bush going to hell and predictions of significant events connected to the end of time taking place in Alaska.

Then too there was the culture of the McCain campaign. Though McCain was personally a Christian who had publicly acknowledged that he was *saved* and *born again*, the manner of his campaign staff was far from anything Palin had experienced among Christian people. There were rough language and hard drinking, violent raging and a hatred for political opponents that bordered on imbalance. From the beginning, Palin had been warned about her *creationism* and told that she ought not make too much of her personal religious life or her religiously inspired views.

She didn't. During the campaign she offered the traditional "God bless America" at the end of her speeches and spoke often of God's grace upon the nation—particularly as a counter to Obama's one-time pastor, Jeremiah Wright, proclaiming that God has "damned" America—but these references were far from what had been her tendency as governor. In other words, she behaved. She reined herself in. She kept faith references to a respectful minimum.

Then the campaign came to an end, and Palin returned to Alaska and began writing *Going Rogue: An American Life*. The very title titillated the faithful. They had sensed that the outspoken governor was overmanaged and manacled during the campaign. They were eager for her to step out on her own, to say the things she had not been allowed to say during all those exhausting, nervously controlled weeks on the campaign trail. Evangelicals in particular began hoping that Palin would cut loose in matters of faith and say what they perceived she had long wanted to say but had discovered was politically incorrect when running for national office. They hoped that the old Sarah might return on the pages of her autobiography, at least in matters of faith.

It was not to be. Oddly, Palin was as circumscribed in religious matters on the pages of *Going Rogue* as she had ever been during the campaign—perhaps even more so. Her description of her conversion experience is a perfect case in point, and in this some context is helpful.

In his 2001 autobiography, George W. Bush went to great lengths to describe his conversion. It was something his family and friends, particularly his mother, had prayed for. As his cousin John Ellis once admitted, George W. Bush was "on the road to nowhere at forty."[4] Part of what plagued Bush was a crisis of comparison, Ellis insists: "You have to really understand how much his father was loved and respected by so many people to understand what it would be like to grow up as a namesake, the son of George Bush. These are the parallels in his life. He went to Andover, went to Yale, went to West Texas, ran for Congress, and at every stage of that he was found wanting. To go through every stage of life and be found wanting and know that people find you wanting, that's a real grind."

Then he found himself on a Maine beach at the family compound in Kennebunkport in 1985 with Billy Graham. As Bush described in *A Charge to Keep*, "It was this beautiful Maine night, and Billy just sat there and talked to us and we asked him questions and shared our thoughts. He and I had a visit afterward—it was just a real personal religious visit—and I started reading the Bible."

This visit was a walk with Graham during which the preacher asked, "Are you right with God?"

"No," Bush replied, "but I want to be." Later he would write, "I was humbled to learn that God sent His Son to die for a sinner like me."[5]

George W. Bush's conversion experience contains all the classic evangelical themes. The convert is a repentant sinner. There is a kind messenger. Sin is exposed, the love of God revealed. And Jesus Christ is known as the savior of sinners through His death on a cross. This was more than religious posturing on Bush's part. It is the experience of millions of Christians who have walked the same path and who have experienced God's grace acting upon the human heart.

Different in kind but similar in transparency is Barack Obama's description of his conversion experience. He had been a South Side Chicago community organizer after graduation from Columbia University but had found it difficult to relate to religious people when he had no faith of his own. As he wrote in *Dreams From My Father*, "Issues, action, power, self-interest. I liked these concepts. They bespoke a certain hardheadedness, a worldly lack of sentiment; politics, not religion."[6]

Still, he was finding his mother's atheism wanting in the face of the heartfelt faith he encountered on Chicago's South Side.

> I had no community or shared traditions in which to ground my most deeply held beliefs. The Christians with whom I worked recognized themselves in me; they saw that I knew their Book and shared their values and sang their songs. But they sensed that a part of me remained removed, *detached*, an observer among them. I came to realize that without a vessel for my beliefs, without an unequivocal commitment to a particular community of faith, I would be consigned at some level to always remain apart, free in the way that my mother was free, but also alone in the same ways she was ultimately alone.[7]

In time, Obama found himself in a pew at Trinity United Church of Christ. Change did not come immediately. He was in a season of wrestling, and had been for some time. Friends had been inviting him to church for months, but he would always demur.

> And I would shrug and play the question off, unable to confess that I could no longer distinguish between faith and mere folly, between faith and simple endurance; that while I believed in the sincerity I heard in their voices, I remained a reluctant skeptic, doubtful of my own motives, wary of expedient conversion, having too many quarrels with God to accept a salvation too easily won.[8]

Finally, the day came. A sermon was preached at Trinity. It was called "The Audacity of Hope." The preacher was the Reverend Doctor Jeremiah Wright. At sermon's end, Obama found himself in tears, and he responded to the call of faith. "It came about as a choice and not an epiphany; the questions I had did not magically disappear. But kneeling beneath that cross on the South Side of Chicago, I felt God's spirit beckoning me. I submitted myself to His will and dedicated myself to discovering His truth."[9]

In later interviews, Obama has said that he has a "personal relationship with Jesus Christ" and he believes "in the redemptive death and resurrection of Jesus Christ...that faith gives me a path to be cleansed of sin and have eternal life."[10]

It was not, perhaps, the traditional evangelical conversion story, but it was specific, and it was a tale told to disclose rather than to obscure.

Now, consider the conversion story of Sarah Palin as recounted in *Going Rogue*.

Remember that Palin is an evangelical, a Pentecostal, in fact. She believes in the death, burial, and resurrection of Jesus Christ. She believes in the powers of the Holy Spirit for the age in which she lives. She believes that the Bible is divinely inspired literature and that its doctrines are truth for all men.

Then, consider her conversion story. She is twelve years old, and she has been at an Assembly of God summer camp. At some point during the experience, she finds herself alone, pondering "the majestic peaks and midnight sun, the wild waters and teeming wildlife."

> I could practically see and hear and feel God's spirit reflected in everything in nature. I reasoned that if God knew what He was doing in this magnificent creation, how much more did He know about me? If He is powerful and wise enough to make all this and thought also to create a speck like me, there surely must be a plan, and He'd know more than I did about my future and my purpose. I made the conscious decision that summer to put my life in my Creator's hands and trust Him as I sought my life's path.[11]

It is important to recall that these are not the words of a twelve-year-old girl or a twenty-year-old mother and wife or a budding politician in her thirties or early forties. These are the words of a woman in her mid-forties who has been governor of a state and who has campaigned for the vice presidency of the United States. We should assume that her portrayal of her conversion is intentional and carefully chosen.

It is also important to recall that Sarah Palin is an intelligent woman. Lay aside for the moment television interviews that did not go well and sometimes clumsy language in public statements. This is a woman who is well read, who has digested C. S. Lewis—arguably the most important Christian apologist of the twentieth century—and who has sat under fine Christian teachers during decades of attending church. She is not theologically unaware, nor can we assume that she is ashamed of her Christian faith.

What then explains this light, even vapid description of perhaps the most important moment in Sarah Palin's life? What explains the difference in detail, theological depth, and transparency between how Palin described her experience and what we've seen of the last two presidents, George W. Bush and Barack Obama? Indeed, if Barack

Obama had described his conversion in such terms, many Americans would have charged that he was a religious liberal attempting a cynical, environmentally friendly attempt to reach to evangelicals.

We can discard the idea that Palin is unaware of what she is doing. She is, again, a theologically astute woman who is religiously certain of herself. This is no mistake, no empty-headed religiosity. Instead, this is Sarah Palin carefully choosing a portrayal of her conversion that will draw as little fire as possible and that will deflect the heat-seeking missiles of anti-evangelicals in American media and society.

It is not hard to understand why. American Christians watched for years as a left-leaning national media bombarded George W. Bush for his faith. Unceasingly, commentators like Lawrence O'Donnell, Chris Matthews, and Rachel Maddow—intriguingly, all of MSNBC—hammered Bush for the presumption of praying in the Oval Office or comforting a soldier at Walter Reed Hospital with a scripture or making public pronouncements of faith. When Palin joined McCain on the Republican ticket in 2008, she became the favorite faith target of a largely anti-Christian media. The assaults became so voracious that author S. E. Cupp felt compelled to write an examination of the media's treatment of religion—Palin's in particular—entitled *Losing Our Religion*. Interestingly, Cupp is an atheist who nevertheless sees the danger of such unvarnished religious bigotry in our national life.

The tragedy of this deference to a secular minority is not only that we lose Palin's full story and what might have been an insightful apologetic for the Christian faith, but also—as this opposition to faith plays out in American culture—that we lose the benefits of faith to the political sphere.

No one wants a theocracy; no one wants the merging of church and state. However, the discerning will want the benefits of traditional faith, as these bring wisdom and morality into play in the political arena. This is the natural, traditional role of religion, for as philosopher George Santayana has written:

It should be observed that, if a systematic religion is true at all, intrusion on its part into politics is not only legitimate, but is the very work it comes into the world to do. Being by hypothesis, enlightened supernaturally, it is able to survey the conditions and consequences of any kind of action much better than the wisest legislature...so that spheres of systematic religion and politics— far from being independent are in principle identical.[13]

Both the American religious Left and the American religious Right are built on this belief, and it is one to be cherished and protected. As Martin Luther King Jr. affirmed:

The church must be reminded that it is not the master or the servant of the state, but rather the conscience of the state. It must be the guide and the critic of the state, and never its tool. If the church does not recapture its prophetic zeal, it will become an irrelevant social club without moral or spiritual authority. If the church does not participate actively in the struggle for peace and for economic and racial justice, it will forfeit the loyalty of millions and cause men everywhere to say that it has atrophied its will. But if the church will free itself from the shackles of a deadening status quo, and, recovering its great historic mission, will speak and act fearlessly and insistently in terms of justice and peace, it will enkindle the imagination of mankind and fire the souls of men, imbuing them with a glowing and ardent love for truth, justice, and peace.[14]

As in so many other arenas, Sarah Palin's presence in American national life exposes fault lines that in turn allow us to ponder our direction as a nation. Her decision to downplay her faith in her biography reveals an understandable response to a voracious anti-religion minority in America. In turn it presses the question of whether Americans wish all religion to be silenced in our public life, or whether, as Dr. King said, religion ought to be the "conscience of the state" in pursuit of "truth, justice, and peace."

Chapter 15

THE POLITICS OF PERSONAL DESTRUCTION

In war you can only be killed once. But in politics many times.

—WINSTON CHURCHILL

THERE IS A VICIOUSNESS RUNNING THROUGH AMERICAN POLI-tics today. It is as though the restraints have been cast off and hatred is now the coin of the public realm. The goal seems to be not merely the defeat of an opponent in the halls of political debate, but the complete destruction of that opponent's reputation, his liveli-hood, and his ability to function in public life.

In a lesser sense, it has always been this way. Earlier in our history, men were nearly caned to death on the floor of Congress, were chal-lenged to duels over political disputes, and had to watch their wives die slow deaths from the poisons spilled out upon them. Newspa-pers served the agendas of political parties by alleging affairs, senility, impotence, financial misdealing, and even heresy on the part of men who were innocent on all counts. This is the grand American tradition of politics as blood sport, and it is, sadly, nothing new in our land.

Yet the devastation seems more severe today, the consequences more widespread. We can remember when Ray Donovan, Ronald

Reagan's secretary of labor, was acquitted of corruption charges after a prolonged trial. On the day of his victory, he stepped to a microphone and famously said, "Where do I go to get my reputation back?"[1] Hundreds of public officials could echo Donovan's words, but, frankly, an elected official is fortunate if all he loses is his reputation. Today the political game is played as a form of total war, and the results are often lost fortunes, destroyed lives, and even prison. Politics now is a bloody arena, and we can be sure that many a man or woman who might have served us well in office has not dared to attempt it for the price it might mean for all they hold dear.

The conventional wisdom is that the new harshness in American politics arose in the wake of Ronald Reagan's appointment of Robert Bork to the Supreme Court. A highly orchestrated, well-financed coalition fought Bork's appointment and did so with such ferocity that even Bork's critics were taken aback. The assaults on Bork reached a crescendo when the late Senator Edward Kennedy attacked Bork on the Senate floor in July of 1987.

> Robert Bork's America is a land in which women would be forced into back-alley abortions, blacks would sit at segregated lunch counters, rogue police could break down citizens' doors in midnight raids, schoolchildren could not be taught about evolution, writers and artists would be censored at the whim of government, and the doors of the federal courts would be shut on the fingers of millions of citizens for whom the judiciary is often the only protector of the individual rights that are the heart of our democracy.[2]

By today's standard, Kennedy's assault was mild. It involved only words. Now the common practice is to attempt to destroy an opponent personally by way of destroying him politically. It is called the *criminalization of politics* or the *politics of personal destruction*. If a man cannot destroy his opponent on the floor of Congress, he instead makes sure this opponent is bombarded with ethics charges and lawsuits. This discredits him before the public—who do not know that an *indictment* or an *ethics probe* might have little to do with guilt or innocence—and so threatens him with financial devastation or criminal sanction that the poor fellow usually leaves office grateful to have escaped worse.

This was the case with Tom DeLay, a Republican House majority leader so effective that Democratic campaign strategist James Carville once said, "If Tom DeLay was a Democrat, we would have control of the House."[3] Yet when DeLay's opponents could not defeat him in the halls of Congress, they decided to destroy him personally. They did this with a storm of ethics charges, lawsuits, and negative media.

In his book *No Retreat, No Surrender*, DeLay describes how in the final twelve years of his more than two decades in office he was tormented by a Democratic leadership intent upon driving him from politics. First there were ethics charges in 1996. These were dismissed. Then, in 1998, more ethics charges. These too were dismissed. Frustrated, DeLay's opposition launched total war. Patrick Kennedy, head of the Democratic Congressional Campaign Committee, engineered a lawsuit against DeLay under RICO—Racketeered Influenced and Corrupt Organizations—laws originally intended to prevent Mafia-style criminal conspiracies. When Nancy Pelosi became House minority leader, she used the power of televised House proceedings to defame DeLay further. More lawsuits soon were filed by organizations like Democracy 21 and Common Cause. Finally, Ronnie Earle, the Democrat district attorney in Travis County, Texas—a DA with a reputation for filing charges against conservative politicians—charged DeLay with money laundering and criminal conspiracy. Distracted and increasingly discredited, DeLay resigned office in mid-2006.[4] As of the writing of this book—five years later—the case against DeLay in Travis County still has not been brought to trial. DeLay remains simply an "indicted former politician."

Nor have these tactics been employed only by the political Left. In a now famously corrupt case, Republican federal attorneys in Alabama engineered charges against former Democratic Governor Don Siegelman that sent both Siegelman and HealthSouth founder Richard Scrushy to federal prison. The case was almost absurd. Scrushy had made a contribution to the Alabama Education Trust that prosecutors insisted was a bribe designed to win an appointment from Siegelman to Alabama's Certificate of Need Review Board, the board that determines where hospitals may be built in Alabama. It did not seem to matter that Scrushy had already been on the Certificate of Need Review Board for nearly two decades. It did not matter that Scrushy had already asked to step down from the board. In a prosecution allegedly orchestrated by Karl Rove, Siegelman and Scrushy were found guilty on June 29, 2006, and Scrushy was sentenced to six years in prison. Oddly, Scrushy is a Republican whose office was adorned with signed pictures of him with recent Republican presidents, all thanking him for his generous contributions to their campaigns. This case was so political and so charged with corruption that fifty-two former state attorneys general urged Congress to investigate.

It should come as no surprise, then, that Sarah Palin received similar treatment. Once she returned to Alaska after the 2008 presidential race, Palin found herself the target of dozens of lawsuits and ethics probes engineered by her political opponents to discredit and so devastate her that she would not return to public life. The variety and pettiness of these charges were astonishing. There was an August 2008 allegation of cronyism in hiring. There were suits alleging that she released protected personnel file information. One lawsuit alleged that she charged the state of Alaska for her children's travel, and another alleged that she campaigned on state property. Oddly, a lawsuit alleged that she participated in the forced drugging of children in state institutions. There was even a suit alleging that she had violated one citizen's civil rights by failing to issue a proclamation in celebration of "Juneteenth," a commemoration of the freeing of U.S. slaves. And Alaskans just shook their heads when they heard that one of the allegations taking up their governor's time was that she had carried a fish away from a lake without having photo identification on her person.

It might all have been a sideshow of American politics had it not been so costly to Palin. Her legal fees threatened to reach $500,000.[5] She was hampered in her ability to focus upon governing her state, and her family was being traumatized by the investigations, the depositions, and the allegations in the press. Finally, after discussing the matter with Todd, the children, and friends, Palin resigned as governor early in July of 2009, with eighteen months remaining in her term. She announced, simply, that she had wearied of "superficial, wasteful political blood sport."[6]

That might have been the end of it. The lies and the suits might have simply gone away, and the Palins might have been allowed to return to their private lives. But Palin was still considered a contender for president in 2012, and so the political hit squads did not stand down. Now the assaults took the form of Internet rumors and lies, and these, of course, threatened to do more damage to Palin's political prospects due to the speed at which they spread and the inability of Palin to counter them when they surfaced. Mark Twain once said, "A lie can travel halfway around the world while the truth is putting on its shoes."[7] By early 2009, Sarah Palin began discovering how true this was.

Yet it was not just the fact of the lie but the brand of the lie used against Palin that is the most revealing part of this tale. Her opponents scanned American culture and realized that the lies that would work best were the ones that painted her as a Bible-thumping religious bigot living at odds with the values she forced on others. Her opponents chose well. It is a caricature that plays effectively to modern stereotypes of people of faith. If Palin could not be driven from office with legitimate criminal charges and lawsuits, and if she could not be discredited in other ways in order to keep her from running in 2012, then painting her as a harsh, narrow-minded, religious hypocrite would get the job done given the prevailing biases in American culture.

The three primary lies alleged of Palin fit this distortion perfectly. There was first the allegation that her baby with Down's syndrome was not hers but her daughter's, and that Sarah had engaged in a huge fraud in order to spare the family shame. Here is a favorite smear: that people of faith are inherently corrupt and that they hypocritically go to great lengths to keep their corruption from the world. The second lie was rooted in a favorite anti-religion canard: that Palin had urged the Wasilla librarian to ban offending books. This fabrication grew from the myth that the religious are inherently anti-intellectual and thus ban books that counter their biases. The final falsehood hurled at Palin was that she believed in a literal and recent six-day Creation. This invention played to the assumption that those who believe in biblical truth must also be antiscientific, and this despite the astonishing contributions of faith to scientific discovery through the years.

It is important, then, to understand a bit more about these three lies in order to understand how they played to prevailing cultural prejudices about people of faith—people of biblical faith in particular.

THE TRUTH ABOUT TRIG

Many Alaskans expressed surprise when, on March 5, 2008, news outlets informed them that their forty-four-year-old governor, who had been in office less than sixteen months, was expecting her fifth child. Their bewilderment is understandable. They were told she was seven months along, and yet they were hearing of the pregnancy for the first time. Indeed, so well had the pregnancy been concealed, the news caught the governor's own staff unaware.

The timing and handling of the late revelation struck some as odd. Brows furrowed. Suspicious minds cogitated. Tongues wagged. Eventually rumors circulated. By the time Trig was born, Alaska's water-cooler gossips and pajama pundits had devised a hypothesis wherein Trig was actually Bristol Palin's baby. The theory was that seventeen-year-old Bristol had turned up pregnant, and Todd and Sarah, desperate to avoid scandal, had convinced their daughter to participate in a charade in which they would tell the world the baby was theirs. For anyone predisposed to dislike the governor, it was a delicious hypothesis.

There were, of course, a few flaws in the conspiracy theory. Those somewhat less prone to believe something ugly about Palin wondered why—if she were going to go to all the trouble of manufacturing a fake pregnancy and thereby risk her entire political future—she would wait until her daughter was seven months pregnant to start the pretense? Why not announce it early and avoid all the shock and suspicion? And why was it *less* embarrassing for a sitting governor to say, "My fellow Alaskans, I've been hiding my pregnancy from you," than having to say, "My unmarried teenage daughter is pregnant"? Alaskans—and Americans as a whole—would have had an easier time understanding the latter than they would the former. The idea of a conspiracy simply made no sense.

The theory suffered another setback when it was learned that Trig was born on April 18, 2008, with Down's syndrome—a condition much more common in babies born to older mothers. In fact, a 2007 study published in the *British Medical Journal* reported that women in their thirties have only a 1-in-940 chance of having a baby with Down's syndrome. But for women in their forties, the chances jump more than tenfold, to 1 in 84.[8]

A third and what should have been fatal blow to the promoters of the "it's Bristol's baby" theory came when it was revealed in August of 2008 that Bristol herself was pregnant and unmarried. She gave birth at full term on December 29, 2008. For those who could do the gestational math, the case was closed. Bristol could not have had a baby in April and then another in December of the same year.

The case should have been closed. However, four months after Trig was born, Sarah was named by John McCain to be his running mate in the presidential contest. A press corps ravenous for information about the largely unknown governor descended upon Alaska, Democratic operatives in tow. Soon, the theories about Trig gained new life on a national scale. *Trig Truthers* have now taken their place in the annals of conspiracy theory lore alongside the *Truthers* who are convinced that 9/11 was an inside job and the *Birthers* who think something is fishy with President Obama's birth certificate, not to mention the *Lunar-tics* who think the Apollo moon landings were faked on a Hollywood soundstage.

At first it was just bloggers, tabloids, and trashy gossip Web sites that were repeating the rumors about Trig. Soon though, more respectable voices joined the chorus of dubious questioners, including *Washington Post* media columnist Howard Kurtz. Joining him was Andrew Sullivan, mentioned in a previous chapter as the writer for *The Atlantic* who called Palin a "pathological liar," "delusional," and "an ignorant nutcase" with regularity. Sullivan's singular fixation has been what he once called "Palin's bizarre story about her fifth campaign prop during the campaign."[9] The "campaign prop" to which Sullivan refers is Trig Palin.

Sullivan's refusal to surrender to common sense and facts has become a source of great mirth for his conservative critics and a source of embarrassment for his liberal allies. Blogger Patrick Frey, a Los Angeles assistant district attorney, has written of Sullivan's obsession with Sarah Palin's uterus. Michelle Malkin has chided Sullivan, calling him *"The Atlantic's* excitable resident womb-chaser."[10] And the gay-centric opinion Web site Queerty has written a piece under the headline "Andrew Sullivan's Sarah Palin Obsession Is Exhausting."[11]

With goading and validation from high-profile media figures like Sullivan, an entire subculture of amateur investigators has sprouted like mushrooms in the darker corners of the Internet. Newswire photographs showing a clearly pregnant Palin are analyzed and dissected like frames from the Zapruder film of the Kennedy assassination. Self-styled experts believe they detect subtle signs of Photoshop alterations in the photographs. Minute details from pictures of newborn Trig are compared with photos taken a few weeks later. It is a subculture all its own.

Those seeking reality have only to walk the streets of Wasilla. There the open-minded find scores of people who saw Palin with child and who watched the pregnancy develop. There are people from churches who attended baby showers and nurses who attended the birth. There are doctors who helped with delivery and even staff members who watched the final months of the pregnancy with joy.

If all this wasn't enough, one of Palin's strongest critics inadvertently provided the best evidence for Palin's version of events. It took the form of an October 2009 *Vanity Fair* interview with Levi Johnston, the young father of Bristol Palin's baby who lived with the Palins for a season prior to Sarah's selection as John McCain's running mate. Perhaps unaware of what he is confirming, Johnston recounted, "Sarah hadn't told us she was pregnant with Trig until about a day or two before she announced it to the media, when she was already seven months pregnant. We saw her getting a little bigger, but she tried to hide it. When we asked her, 'You're pregnant, aren't you?' she denied it. Finally, one day Willow was going through things in Sarah's room and stumbled across a pregnancy test and said, 'Mom, what's this?' Sarah finally came out and said she was pregnant."[12] Whatever else Johnston's interview alleges, it makes clear that Sarah Palin was pregnant with the child who was eventually named Trig.

The lie about Trig Palin being Bristol's child rather than her mother's draws strength from a vile assumption about people of faith. It is a lie rooted in the ideas of Sigmund Freud and developed by philosophers like Ludwig Andreas Feuerbach and Karl Marx. It is that shame is at the heart of religion, that religion is a man-made device for ameliorating the guilt that human beings feel when they commit acts for which they feel guilt. This is the belief that has moved so many Trig Palin conspiracy theorists to rush to judgment in the face of overwhelming facts to the contrary.

The theory is simple: Sarah Palin is religious. Shame is at the foundation of all religion. Palin found her daughter to be with child. Rather than acknowledge the truth and face the shame of her daughter's misdeeds, Palin perpetrated a massive fraud. This is the manner of the religious.

It could not be that a mother was devastated by the news of being pregnant with a child with Down's syndrome and needed time to adjust. It could not be that this was private business and the outer world could wait. It could not be that Palin needed the news to remain between her and her husband for a while before she had to help her wider family adjust. No, Palin lied about Trig, and this is what people of faith do.

Thus the conspiracy theories. Thus the allegations. Thus a portrayal of Palin that American culture could easily believe.

THE TRUTH ABOUT BOOK BANNING

Other common Palin myths are far less serious than accusations of faking a pregnancy and are easier to address. One of the favorite themes of Palin's most ardent bashers is that she had numerous books banned from the Wasilla library after becoming mayor there. Other rumors claim that she merely *attempted* to have books banned but failed.

Much of the stir over this lie came from an e-mail that has been endlessly forwarded since Palin became a national figure and that provides great detail about how Palin tried to have books removed from the library. Included is a list of more than ninety supposedly banned books. This much-circulated e-mail claims that its information comes directly from the "official minutes of the Wasilla Library Board."

The e-mail is a lie of the type possible in an Internet age, one that gains strength by breadth of distribution rather than accuracy. Sincere Internet attempts to counter the lie—such as at Snopes .com—have been unable to correct the damage done. This is the case despite the fact that Snopes.com has proven that some of the books Palin was supposed to have banned were not even in print when she was in office.

The truth, attested to by numerous sources and parties involved, is that shortly after becoming mayor, Palin asked the librarian how she would handle a challenge from a citizen about a given book. It was a question first raised by one of Palin's constituents, which she then asked of the librarian. The librarian told Palin that she would oppose the removal of any book from the library just because one or more people found the content offensive. Palin accepted her answer and nothing further was said. Like the lie about Trig Palin's birth, this allegation of book banning would have died a natural death had it not fit a culture-wide misunderstanding of biblical faith.

THE TRUTH ABOUT PALIN AND ORIGINS

The third of these revealing lies about Palin relates to the evolution/Creation debate. Intriguingly, what keeps the lies in circulation is not only a cultural bias about the antiscientific beliefs of people of faith but also Palin's own balanced views on the issue, which defy easy categorization.

There is a widely held assumption on the part of non-Christians that taking the Bible seriously requires a belief that the earth is only about six thousand years old. This isn't the case. There is indeed a subset of Christians who hold to a conviction that the six "days" of Creation mentioned in the first chapter of Genesis are literal, twenty-four-hour days and that there are no large gaps in the Creation narrative. This subset is often called "young Earth creationists."

There is also a large and growing segment of Christians who see no fundamental conflict between the Genesis account and the geological record that testifies of an earth that is billions of years old. Palin is solidly in this camp.

Whenever asked by a reporter about her views on teaching evolution in the public schools, Palin has asserted that the best science available ought to be taught in the classroom, just as her father did during his career. She has also said that she would prefer that school children at least be exposed to the arguments for Intelligent Design—the idea that there is some form of intelligent *Creator* behind the origin of life and the universe—and that they are at least made aware of the Creation/evolution debate. "I don't think there should be a prohibition against debate if it comes up in class," she told a reporter for the *Anchorage Daily News* in 2006 when running for governor. "It doesn't have to be part of the curriculum." In that interview she added that, if elected, she would not push the state Board of Education to add such Creation-based material to the state's required curriculum.[13]

And she didn't. It was a balanced, principled stand that defied the caricatures and that showed a statesman-like deference to both science and traditional faith.

Though the above are the archetypical lies alleged of Palin, and for largely religious reasons, there is a broader charge that has also received currency. It is perhaps best summarized in this quote from a comment thread at a popular blog: "If Sarah Palin is elected president, they will be burning books, arresting women who abort, and rounding up homosexuals into detention camps."[14] The broader issue is whether Palin aspires to be a religious dictator if elected to higher office or whether she will submit to the rule of the law of the land.

Thankfully, we do not have to guess. We have specific evidence from Palin's time as governor of Alaska. A single example will tell the tale.

One of Palin's first acts as governor was to veto a piece of legislation she would have preferred to sign. In 2005, Alaska's highest court had ruled that the state government's practice of denying benefits to the same-sex partners of state employees violated Alaska's constitution. Palin disagreed with the ruling and said so publicly. When she did, she spoke as a private citizen in Wasilla following her resignation from the Alaska Oil and Gas Conservation Commission. Few were surprised. Palin did not and does not support redefining marriage or much else identified with the gay rights agenda.

By the time she reached the governor's mansion, however, the Alaska state legislature had passed a bill that reversed the state court's ruling. Palin was sympathetic to the aims of the bill, but her attorney general advised her that it was unconstitutional, that it violated the constitution's separation of powers provisions. Palin studied the issue and agreed.

Over cries of protest from her own base of support, she vetoed the bill. It was a courageous stand but one perfectly consistent with her pattern of loyalty to principle above all—constitutional principle in particular.

This and a number of other episodes like it ought to have satisfactorily answered the question about Palin's commitment to the rule of law. It did not, both because her critics were ignorant of the facts and because they were too wedded to outworn assumptions about faith and its oppressive role in the public square.

There is little sign of the politics of personal destruction ceasing to devastate our national life anytime soon. Instead, political bombardments have become even more widespread, the tactics used by political opponents against each other even more insidious and cruel. We should hope for a better day.

What is important about the tactics used against Sarah Palin is not just that they are lies without foundation, but that they are lies based upon popular assumptions about faith that are alive and well in the popular mind today. The truth is that Americans are schooled in antireligion bigotry from an early age, and then these distortions are reinforced by popular media throughout their lives. Such falsehoods fuel a politics of hate and manipulation, and it is time for a discerning people to recognize this and set themselves to reform.

Chapter 16

PALIN AND THE FRONTRUNNERS FOR 2012

I guess this is just another lost cause, Mr. Paine. All you people don't know about lost causes. Mr. Paine does. He said once they were the only causes worth fighting for.
—JEFFERSON SMITH
in *Mr. Smith Goes to Washington*

ROUGHLY ONE HUNDRED FIFTY PROTESTERS ARE JOSTLING for position outside the Hilton Hotel in downtown Eugene, Oregon. It is April 23, 2010, and Sarah Palin is scheduled to speak at a Lincoln Day fund-raiser for the Lane County Republican Party there. The event has been sold out since shortly after tickets went on sale.

Some outsiders are surprised to learn there even *is* a Republican Party in Lane County. Eugene is an overwhelmingly liberal town in a liberal state. It is also a state college town—the home of the University of Oregon—which tends to pull the political center of gravity even further to the left. Nevertheless, the populist and conservative undercurrents that have been transforming the political landscape since shortly after the election of Barack Obama are being felt here too. A Tea Party Tax Day rally three weeks earlier drew more than one thousand—surprising many long-time observers of the political scene.[1]

Two protest signs outside the Hilton this day offer an interesting contrast of sentiments. The first is a handmade sign that reads "Eugene: A Hate Free Zone." It is safe to assume the holder viewed Palin as a purveyor of hate. The second sign, positioned to the right and just behind the first, reads "I Hope She Chokes." The "o" in *chokes* is the familiar circular logo of the Obama campaign. Clearly, *hate* is as malleable a concept in Eugene as it seems to be everywhere else in America these days.

Inside, Palin is warmly received and enthusiastically cheered by a crowd of hundreds. Some observers wondered aloud, "If Sarah Palin can draw an enthusiastic crowd in Eugene, where can she *not* fill a hall?"

After the 2008 election—the one that put Barack Obama in the White House and strengthened the hands of Nancy Pelosi and Harry Reid by increasing their majorities in the House and Senate—many described the Republican Party as irreparably broken and heading for long-term decline. In two consecutive elections, the Republicans had lost ground in every significant category. In addition to losing the White House and seats in both houses of Congress, they lost governorships and dozens of seats in state legislatures as well.

The laws of human nature suggest that after every setback or disaster comes a wave of blame fixing and finger pointing. Where the fault lay for the Republicans' decline depended upon who was speaking and who their favorite bogeyman happened to be. For many inside and outside of the party, though, that favorite bogeyman was the *religious Right*.

"The Christian Right Killed the Republican Party" declared a columnist for the *Huffington Post*.[2] *Newsweek*'s editors shook their heads and collectively declared "The End of Christian America."[3] And Max Blumenthal, a writer for the leftist magazine *The Nation* and a harsh critic of evangelical Christianity, rushed a book to press breathlessly entitled *Republican Gomorrah: Inside the Movement That Shattered the Party*.[4] Blumenthal's book took particular pains to hold up McCain's risky selection of Sarah Palin as a spectacular example of how catering to the demands of social conservatives was a prescription for Republican defeat.

The preferred narrative was simple: "The Republican Party must once and for all divorce itself from conservative evangelicals and Catholics if it ever hopes to appeal to the emerging new majority of postmodern skeptics, libertarians, and especially, the more *enlightened* and *sophisticated* urban voters on the coasts."

In other words, "Stop opposing abortion, gay marriage, illegal immigration, and gun control." This was the gist of the advice coming from conservative pundits such as David Frum and *New York Times* columnist David Brooks—people who sincerely want to see the Republican Party prosper. Oddly enough, this was the same advice being offered by the likes of Max Blumenthal, who would just as soon see the Republican Party disappear.

This advice seems odd given how the issues that define the Republican Party tend to poll with the American electorate at large. The nation is evenly divided on abortion, but the trends favor the pro-life cause, particularly among young people. Large majorities oppose gay marriage in every part of the country, with even progressive California passing Proposition 8—an anti-gay marriage initiative—while voting for Barack Obama overwhelmingly. Likewise, proposals to secure the borders and reduce illegal immigration are broadly supported by the electorate in nearly every region of the United States. And there is little interest in tighter gun control laws outside of a handful of urban centers.

Looking back on the 2008 election, Republican defeat seems to have sprung from five overwhelming forces.

1. The astonishing popularity of Barack Obama
2. Popular disgust with the Bush administration
3. A historic economic crisis
4. A dramatic shift of faith-based voters toward the left
5. The rise of new millennial voters and their unique political pastiche

None of these factors demand that Republicans abandon their core principles in order to win elections. Yet, what if they did? What if the Republican Party were to heed the prevailing view and eject the faith-based and the traditionalists from their party? Their numbers would be replaced and expanded upon by precisely...whom? The 10 to 20 percent of voting-age Americans who can be considered *libertarians* isn't a large enough group with which to win victories.[5] Besides, about half of these are already holding their noses and voting Republican as the lesser of two evils. Divorcing the nation's conservative Christians seems a questionable strategy, since they are more than a third of the party base. This would be a risky strategy, perhaps even a *devil's bargain* wherein the party sells its very soul for an illusory promise.

This fear and scrambling for answers were understandable, though. Matters were bleak for Republicans the morning after the 2008 elections. Some jubilant Democrats were even proclaiming that America had just witnessed a historic, once-in-a-generation *realignment* of the electorate, similar to the one heralded by the election of Ronald Reagan in 1980.

Predictions such as these quickly proved false, however. In fact, these theories did not even survive the first year of the Obama administration. By the end of 2009, it was clear that reports of the death of the Republican Party had been greatly exaggerated, as Republicans won gubernatorial special elections in Virginia and New Jersey and even in New England states. At the same time, in small towns and in major cities across the land, average Americans filled raucous town hall meetings, and thousands turned out for Tea Party protests—including in unlikely places like Boston.

In January, Republican Scott Brown's effort to fill the late Senator Edward Kennedy's Senate seat in Massachusetts sent shockwaves through America's political class. When the pickup-driving, Tea Party–friendly Brown won, pundits were stunned, and predictions of Republican demise fell flat.

Max Blumenthal had called the Christian Right "the movement that shattered" the Republican Party. But by the middle of 2010, the party wasn't looking very shattered. In fact, by the end of the spring of 2010, Democratic insiders and analysts were issuing dire warnings that there was no longer any such thing as a safe seat for Democrats anywhere in America. Nearly every congressional seat on the map was in play for the Republicans, and the *movement*, which was supposedly exerting a boat-anchor-like drag on the ship of Republican prospects, turned out to be an engine of propulsion instead.

Then in May 2010, matters grew even worse for the political Left. Conservatives began winning critical elections. In Hawaii, Republican Charles Djou won a special House election and became the first Republican to hold the 1st District in twenty years. This victory held particular symbolic value since the district Djou now represents is the one in which Barack Obama grew up. Rand Paul, son of one-time Libertarian presidential candidate and Texas congressman Ron Paul, celebrated victory in a Tea Party–inspired Senate primary race in Kentucky. Equally symbolic, Senator Arlen Specter, a Republican for six terms who switched to the Democrat Party in 2009, lost his primary race. Even Republicans were not immune to this trend. Bob Bennett of Utah—long a centrist Republican in the Senate—lost his primary race to a Tea Party–backed candidate, and largely because he had voted for Obama's stimulus package. Clearly, the mood of the country was turning conservative and anti-incumbent, and Republicans saw in this a restoration of their fortunes.

At the forefront of both the Tea Party movement and this popular grassroots backlash was Sarah Palin. She had sensed this rising tide and had not been caught unprepared. In fact, by the middle of 2010, she had put in place the networking that she hoped would lead her to greater political impact.

While she crisscrossed the country speaking at fund-raising events for fellow Republicans, she also started her own political action committee, SarahPAC, which allowed her to contribute to the campaigns of friends or even to her own cause, should she run again. She began communicating with her supporters through Twitter and Facebook, accumulating more than 137,000 *followers* on the former and more than a million and a half *fans* on the latter. She signed a deal with The Learning Channel to host a television series featuring Alaska's natural beauty, and she signed a book deal for a follow-up to *Going Rogue* called *America From the Heart*, an exploration of patriotic themes, poetry, and lore. Palin also became a commentator for FOX News and host of a periodic FOX series called *Real American Stories*.

In other words, Palin did what politicians aspiring to run for president do between elections. She broadened her base. She kept herself in the public eye. She extended her brand. She fine-tuned her positions. She sharpened her skills.

Still, she knows that if she runs for national office again she will have an uphill fight. At the 2010 Conservative Political Action Convention (CPAC) in February, a straw poll of presidential preferences among the registered attendees put Palin, at 7 percent, a fairly distant third behind Texas congressman Ron Paul (31 percent) and former Massachusetts governor Mitt Romney (22 percent).[6] This showing was slightly better, however, than that of Newt Gingrich or Mike Huckabee, who each got 4 percent of the votes.

The CPAC poll was not the only indicator that Palin has a long, tall hill to climb if she has her eye on the White House. At roughly the same time that the CPAC attendees were casting their straw poll ballots, the results of a *Washington Post*–ABC News poll were announced. The news wasn't good for the former governor.

> Although Palin is a Tea Party favorite, her potential as a presidential hopeful takes a severe hit in the survey. Fifty-five percent of Americans have unfavorable views of her, while the percentage holding favorable views has dipped to 37, a new low in Post-ABC polling.
>
> There is a growing sense that the former Alaska governor is not qualified to serve as president, with more than seven in 10 Americans now saying she is unqualified, up from 60 percent in a November survey. Even among Republicans, a majority now say Palin lacks the qualifications necessary for the White House.[7]

Clearly, Palin has been hurt in popular perception by her resignation as Alaska's governor, by her poor performances in critical interviews, and by the possibility that she is an opportunist who has hitched her star to the Tea Party movement. Still, it would be a mistake to underestimate her potential. She looked equally dead politically after she resigned from the Alaska Oil and Gas Conservation Commission. Two years later she was putting the state jet up for sale on eBay.

Should she decide to run for president, she will have to master an impressive Republican field. The leading contender is likely Mitt Romney. He will be a formidable foe. He is handsome, well spoken, and polished. He looks like he is straight from central casting, as does his family. He has run an automobile company, rescued an Olympics, and been the successful governor of a bellwether state. Nearly as important, he is wealthy and will have no problem funding a presidential run.

Romney's primary problem will be his faith, as surprising as this may be in our day. He is a Mormon, and this religion is still misunderstood and suspected in American culture. A Rasmussen survey in 2006 asked evangelicals whether or not they could ever vote for a person of the Mormon faith for president. At that time, 53 percent answered, "No."[8] Still, it may be that this reluctance has eroded significantly in the intervening years. The fact that a group called *Evangelicals for Romney* was highly visible at a number of Republican events in 2010 could be a sign that this is the case.

Romney's other problem will be the charge that he is not sufficiently conservative. Romney helped design a health care plan for Massachusetts when he was governor of that state that has been described as a model for Barack Obama's approach to health care. This will not help Romney if the national mood continues to swing to the right. Nor will he appeal to conservatives if much is made of the fact that he has come newly to his pro-life views, that when he was Massachusetts's governor his health care plan increased state-funded abortions and appointed Planned Parenthood as an overseer of procedures. This history can be lived down, of course, but it will be more difficult the more rightward the country drifts prior to 2012.

In his favor is the fact that Romney is conservative enough to suit Sarah Palin. While speaking at a Boston Tax Day rally on April 15, 2010, Palin was asked if she would consider being Romney's running mate. "Sounds good to me," she responded.[9]

If the CPAC straw poll is any guide, Palin would also have to surpass Ron Paul. Given the national mood, it would seem that his day has come. He is a philosophical libertarian and has wide respect in that camp despite his pro-life views. He is also a virtual grandfather of the Tea Party movement, which is currently having such electoral success. Paul is a strict constitutionalist at a time when constitutional constraints are a front-burner topic. He is also a physician when health care and medical matters will be consuming national issues for years to come. And he has proven himself capable of raising funds, having broken records for Internet contributions during the election of 2008.

Yet Paul has seldom faired well in national elections. He has the air of the quirky professor, and this sometimes does not translate well in media. He is also hesitant to discuss his faith, and in a field likely populated by Romney and Palin, this will be a disadvantage. On this, Paul has said:

> I have never been one who is comfortable talking about my faith in the political arena. In fact, the pandering that typically occurs in the election season I find to be distasteful. But for those who have asked, I freely confess that Jesus Christ is my personal Savior, and that I seek His guidance in all that I do. I know, as you do, that our freedoms come not from man, but from God. My record of public service reflects my reverence for the Natural Rights with which we have been endowed by a loving Creator.[10]

Paul may also be disadvantaged with faith-based voters by several of his policy positions. He is opposed to all foreign aid—including aid to Israel—opposed to most aspects of the war on terror, supports the decriminalization of narcotics, and advocates a complex approach to the issues surrounding gay marriage.

Nevertheless, if there was ever a presidential election in which a Ron Paul could gain his party's nomination, it is the one looming in 2012. There is a liberal in the White House whose policies are proving unpopular and ineffective. The most effective movement on the right, the Tea Party movement, is virtually his creation. His America-first, Constitution-only approach to politics has high appeal. He is also pro-life as the nation is turning in that direction and pro-limited government when the country is weary of the burdens of the state. Paul will find a hearing if not a victory in 2012, and Palin will have to engage his ideas if she hopes to win.

The third possible opponent for Palin according to the CPAC poll is Newt Gingrich. He too will be a difficult man to defeat. As a former Speaker of the House, Gingrich is experienced in national politics as few men are. He is articulate, intelligent, well spoken, and media savvy. In the first three months of 2010, he raised more money for his PAC than Mitt Romney, Governor Tim Pawlenty, Mike Huckabee, and Sarah Palin combined. As one popular liberal blogger phrased it, "Anyone who thinks Newt Gingrich isn't positioning himself for a run at the Republican nomination isn't paying attention."[11]

Yet Gingrich's flaws could damage his run for the White House. He is an intellectual who is ever thinking great thoughts but who is seldom able to translate those thoughts into real-world action. Both Tom DeLay and Dick Armey left office complaining of this. Both men believed the Republican Revolution of 1994 would have lived longer had Gingrich not been so quixotic. He will have to prove that he has risen above this to win the nomination.

Moreover, he will have to rise above his messy personal life. He has had numerous divorces and an affair. It was widely rumored that he divorced one of his wives while she lay in a hospital dying of cancer. In an election in which values and faith are likely to play a heightened role, this will not serve Gingrich well.

He has given evidence of change, though. He was a Baptist for most of his adult life, but in March of 2009, he quietly converted to

Catholicism. In an interview with *Christianity Today* not long after, Gingrich spoke openly about his faith.

> It's hard for me to imagine as a person of faith how it would not impact your policies. In the end, if you truly try to understand what God wants, and truly try to do what God wants, that has to impact how you behave.
>
> It's undoubtedly made me much more pro-life. It's undoubtedly made me more concerned about young people learning about God, learning a sense of being part of an extended world. I think that it makes me much more concerned about helping the poor.[12]

In the same interview he was asked about Sarah Palin and his view of her political prospects. He expressed admiration but also reservations about her readiness:

> She is probably the most successful figure in the party right now, and she's a formidable figure. I think to go from there to becoming a national leader would take a significant amount of work.[13]

Gingrich has perhaps said it well. If Sarah Palin intends to seek the presidency, it will require work and discipline beyond what she has known. She will have to prove that she is no longer a lightweight, no longer the air-headed Republican darling of 2008. She can do it, and many hope she will, but it will be one of the great transformations in the history of American politics.

There is another option for her, and it is certain she is considering this path as well. She may run not to win but by way of running for power, by way of seeking a larger slice of the political pie. There are many who have done it. Al Sharpton and Jesse Jackson never actually thought they would win the presidency when they ran. They were simply running for greater visibility, perhaps a wider recognition for their values and their cause. It worked for them, and Palin may do the same. She may run knowing that she will never achieve the White House, but knowing too that it will raise the volume of her conservative voice and give her a broader platform for both her politics and her celebrity brand.

What is certain is that Sarah Palin will have to change, have to evolve, have to morph into the weightier statesman of her dreams in order to continue to play a role in American political life. Whether she will do this, or whether she will merely settle into her current cult of personality, remains to be seen.

Section 3 Afterword

SEVEN THINGS SARAH PALIN NEEDS TO KNOW

Character is destiny.
—HERACLITUS

S HE HAS BECOME ONE OF THE MOST VISIBLE POLITICAL FIGURES of our generation. She has electrified much of the conservative portion of the American political spectrum, a movement that had been nearly cast adrift before her arrival on the national scene. Her speeches draw larger crowds than do those of any other U.S. politician except Barack Obama, and her autobiography, *Going Rogue: An American Life*, sold millions of copies, breaking sales records for its genre. Just as important, she is young, eager to make her mark, and she has achieved that status that trumps all others in American society: celebrity. She will play a decisive role in our nation for years to come.

Yet she has stepped onto the stage of American life with a relatively thin résumé for the influence she now holds. She was mayor of Wasilla, Alaska—a town of four thousand—for less than six years and was the governor of that state for barely three. This is to take nothing away from her accomplishments, but it is instructive to keep in mind that her ascent has been rapid and her time for reflection has been slight.

There are truths, then, that she may have missed, or that in the speed of her current life she may not have fully grasped. It may be helpful to ponder these for a moment and to hope that she too finds opportunity to do the same.

1. Love ennobles politics.

This may seem a sickly sweet, syrupy thing to say. It may sound too much like Bill and Hillary Clinton's *politics of meaning* or George H. W. Bush's *thousand points of light*. They are the kind of phrases that speechwriters love for their euphony but which fall empty upon the public's ears. To speak of love anywhere in the proximity of politics may simply sound like more of the same.

Yet all statesmen who are serious about leading well, who are intent upon leaving a lasting impact upon society, must find their highest, most genuine politics. They must sort through the popular rhetoric just as they sort through the crowded rooms of their own inner lives to discover the linear connection between their times, the needs of those they serve, their skills, and the political passions of their heart. This is how statecraft grows from soul craft.

It does not require an exhaustive review of Sarah Palin's political career to discover that she is at her best when she is leading out of love. Her best speeches grow from her love for Alaska and her people. Her most dramatic acts of service have come from a desire to end the corruption that grew like a cancer on the civic body she loves. She has shown herself most noble in the care of her family, in her welcoming of a special needs child, in her honor for her friends. All of this is about love.

From the time of John McCain's summons, Palin has been on the attack. This is what that critical moment in the 2008 election required, what Republicans were desperate for, and what wrung the most thrilling response from the crowds. Palin rose to the call. She transformed bedeviling Obama's every act into an art form and later served both John McCain's senatorial race and the Tea Party movement with large doses of well-crafted venom.

There is more to her than this, though, and she must rediscover it for herself before the clock runs out on her current plan of assault. She knows what love is. She grew up in a loving home and entered public life largely for what she held dear rather than for whom she wanted to destroy. She must recover this inspiration and do it now, remembering that while politicians carp and spat for a season, the work of statesmen endures for generations, ennobled by love of truth and love of those they serve.

2. Hang a lantern on your weaknesses.

It is perhaps too much to expect genuine humility from politicians. They arrive at their heights by fiercely believing in themselves, and it is not surprising that this should sometimes bleed over into pride and even arrogance. Tending these weeds in a politician's soul is a matter for a spouse, close friends, and clergy. The public, however, should not be surprised that their leaders are flawed in such a way. Even Winston Churchill once wrote to his wife, "I am so devoured by egoism that I would like to have another soul in another world and meet you in another setting."[1] It should come as no surprise that the lesser lights of our own day might feel much the same.

Yet there is a bit of wisdom that has come down through the years and that, if not a fruit of character, ought to at least be a tactic of self-preservation for public figures. It is this: hang a lantern on your weaknesses.

The smart politician describes his faults before his enemies get a chance. He admits his failings with a laugh before his opponents have opportunity to portray those failings in dark and dangerous terms. This is a means of not only disarming the opposition but also of endearing oneself to a forgiving and similarly flawed public.

There is a case in point to be imagined from the life of George W.

Bush. It was widely known that he was beset with some syndrome of verbal confusion. Some experts said he was an undiagnosed dyslexic. He was famous for mangling terms like *strategery* and for summoning his listeners to choose *the high horse or the low road*. This weakness on the part of the sitting president was a raucous playground for late-night comics, but it was a serious inability to communicate that tragically damaged his presidency.

Suppose he had decided to hang a lantern on his weaknesses. Suppose that rather than cover his inabilities he had decided to be tested, admitted publicly that he had wrestled with a minor form of dyslexia all his life, and committed himself to address the issue? How this might have endeared him to an American society ever cheering for the underdog. How this would have made his rise to the presidency seem an even more astonishing feat. And what might this have meant for dyslexic school children the world over that an American president faced similar challenges?

This is a lesson that Sarah Palin must absorb. She has built her public success on her *Sarah Barracuda* reputation, on the strength of an inner force that blows past failings and flaws as though they do not exist. But this is unwise in public life, particularly in a media age where every blemish and discoloration is transmitted in high definition. Better the knowing laugh, the homey expression of self-deprecation, the confession of weaknesses the world already sees. This will require a new skill set for Sarah Palin, and it will feel awkward and unnatural for a time. But it is more than posturing. It is the fruit of wisdom and a reaching for humility that at least reflects a respect for virtue if it is not a virtue in itself.

3. Do not run away from faith. Articulate it.

It is conventional wisdom in some quarters that politicians should de-emphasize their religious lives in deference to a secular society. This reasoning contends that the public wants to know that its leaders have a meaningful faith, thus assuring lofty values and morality, but that they don't want that faith to be too visible. This view has led many politicians to publicly distance themselves from their most cherished beliefs, and it may have moved Sarah Palin to downplay her faith to the point of extremes in her autobiography, *Going Rogue*, as we have seen.

There is a counter argument, though, that the public is eager to know what their leaders actually believe but are nervous about unexplained religious platitudes. When George W. Bush said that his favorite political philosopher is Jesus Christ "because He changed my heart," and yet let this stand without explanation, the public was left wondering how this private belief might shape the life of the nation. When Ronald Reagan began pondering the eventuality of Armageddon, the conflagration that some students of the Bible believe will bring history to a violent end, many Americans were naturally concerned about what he might conclude. And Jimmy Carter spoke of being "born again" but took no pains to explain what this might mean for his role in the White House.

The lesson is not that modern politicians should run away from their faith. The lesson is that modern politicians should explain their faith and what it might mean for their conduct in office. Sarah Palin is uniquely equipped for this. Despite negative press to the contrary, she is a well-read, well-pastored, well-taught evangelical who could easily articulate the meaning of her brand of faith for public policy. She should turn from the dumbed-down approach she chose in *Going Rogue* and become the articulate evangelical politician that she is perfectly positioned to be.

4. Dare to grow.

It was hard to watch. In a January 2010 interview, FOX news star Glenn Beck asked Sarah Palin a simple question: "Who is your favorite founder?"

Palin, flustered, answered, "You know, well, all of them because they came collectively together with so much diverse..."

Beck interrupted. "Bull crap," he said. "Who is your favorite?"

Palin kept going. "...so much diverse opinion and so much diversity in terms of belief, but collectively they came together...and they were led by, of course George Washington, so he's got to rise to the top."[2]

It was not the first time that Sarah Palin had flubbed an interview and by her own admission. Yet this one, and all the ones before, provided her with an opportunity: Grow. Deepen. Increase. Right there in public view. Read and learn and broaden and put the fruit of it on public display.

There are those who will urge her otherwise. Some in American politics believe that it is best to stay in the shallow end of the pool. It is safe there and free of embarrassment. There is no need to admit that there are things you don't know. Cover your ignorance, and charge your staff to make sure your lack of knowledge is never exposed.

Yet this approach is not befitting a serious leader who intends to effect profound change. It is also not worthy of Sarah Palin. She should draw from her strengths. She is an aggressive reader, and she retains what she learns. This is her heritage. She should build on it. She should read and let the public hear about it. She should consider an Oprah-like, conservative book club, and so become identified with great literature and great ideas. She could even call the occasional summit of notable conservative minds and tell them, "Look, I've been in public office for more than a decade, and I don't know some of the things I should. Many Americans probably feel the same way. Let's talk about the seminal ideas and solutions for our time."

There is no shame in not knowing. There is even no shame in not answering well. There is shame, though, in not knowing or answering well the second time around.

5. Critics are not enemies.

We have all had this experience. We are listening to a speaker who has been stung by a critical word. He is hurt, enflamed. He uses his speech to strike back. He hits hard and does not let up. But he is talking past us. We do not know what has been said, and we do not understand why we are subjected to this angry tirade. Moreover, rather than being impressed with the persuasiveness of his argument, we leave more impressed with how small and vain this man is. He has lost us, and all because he could not rise above, could not let criticism go unanswered and unavenged.

It was the great missionary statesman E. Stanley Jones who said, "My critics are the unpaid guardians of my soul."[3] It is a truth that would serve Sarah Palin well. There is wisdom to be heard in the mouths of one's enemies, and she would be well served by knowing it. Critics hold up a mirror we would not otherwise see, allow us a clarified view of ourselves that we cannot get any other way. We have to discriminate, of course, and pick out the diamonds of wisdom from the dunghill of hate. Still, there is truth to be had, and the wise leader learns to face criticism, discover the truth in it, and change accordingly. It distinguishes greatness from vanity and rage, carefully crafted performance from genuine largeness of heart. Sarah Palin is capable of these, but only if she refuses to be embittered by those who strike at her.

6. The poor, the needy, and minorities are conservative concerns too.

It is an oddity of modern politics that while conservatives believe they have the solutions for the poor and underprivileged, they seldom mention them. Conservatives prefer to speak in general terms about a healthy economy, about opportunities to achieve, and about the character that leads to prosperity, but rarely do they mention the poor, the disadvantaged, or people of color. It as though they believe that to mention them is to play into liberal hands. What they end up doing, though, is losing the battle in the popular mind by yielding the high ground of compassion and benevolence to their opponents.

Sarah Palin knows better. She comes from a family that, while far from poverty, fought hard to meet daily needs. Both her parents

worked a variety of jobs to serve the family, and the Heath obsession with hunting was about more than sport. It was about feeding
six hungry mouths. Then, when she married, she lived on a blue-
collar workman's salary and often struggled to make ends meet. In
her family experience and in decades of life in the Mat-Su Valley, she
has seen want and poverty, and she knows what can lead to both. She
can connect these issues to conservative answers in a manner that
few politicians today are able to achieve.

She has also lived close to the issue of race. She is married to a man
from a minority group: Todd is a Yupik Eskimo. She has governed
minorities with success in a state where government is forced to deal
with native issues as much as in any other state in the union. She
has also taken note of Republican failings in this arena. George W.
Bush was far from a racist—indeed, he had the most racially diverse
cabinet in American history up to his time, and he even had minorities in his family—yet his refusal to speak to NAACP conferences
and to address issues of race in any meaningful terms allowed opponents to paint Bush as a typical, white, country-club insulated racist.
It wasn't true, but the nearly inarticulate Bush White House was
powerless to counter this slur. Palin could do better.

She should break out of the Republican manner of years and
become a champion of conservative solutions for the poor and an
advocate for racial equality. She should reintroduce words like *poverty*,
needy, *hurting*, and *inequality* to the Republican lexicon and prove the
power of non-statist solutions for our world's most desperate needs.
As a mother, as an oil field worker's wife, and as a woman who has
been willing to know and love the destitute and the non-white, she is
qualified to do—and perhaps courageous enough to do—what most
politicians on the right are not: challenge the political Left on the
home turf of underprivileged and non-white America.

7. Know your boundaries.

Sarah Palin is a woman of Scripture, and so she knows the appealing words of Psalm 16: "The boundary lines have fallen for me in pleasant places."[4] They are words that suggest the contentment, the effectiveness, and the peace of living within one's range of abilities. It is a truth she should grasp anew as she steps on the stage of whatever is next for her in life.

Most people who become prominent reached their position by challenging barriers. They are African Americans who defied racism or women who challenged glass ceilings or the many who overcame some potentially defining flaw in their lives. They are not cowards, and they are not weaklings. They have known their battles.

Yet one of the great lessons of their victories should be the power of concentrated force. You do not break through by applying strength broadly. You penetrate at a defined point. You force through at a pinprick, and then you broaden once you have broken out to the other side.

Many who have reached prominence have not learned this. They interpret their victories as an affirmation of their strength in all things. Rather than learning their lane and gaining a clear understanding of their boundaries, they overreach and attempt what is not theirs to achieve.

Sarah Palin has done this. She is a gifted woman who has had much success, and this could leave her with the sense that she should charge Sarah Barracuda-like into realms that are not hers. It would not serve her well, as her embarrassing television interviews have shown. Yet, if she could take stock of her strengths and gain a clear understanding of what she is not gifted to do, she could engage the challenges of American society where she can do the most good.

The alternative is a messiah complex. It is believing oneself the answer to all things, assuming that there is no realm that should go unchallenged. But this leads to defeat and distraction from the few arenas in which victory could be sweet and meaningful.

There is good to come from Sarah Palin's presence on our national stage, but only if she confines herself to those realms for which her life and her principles have prepared her.

It was the ancient Greeks who eagerly stressed the message that "character is destiny," and this is the lesson—and all of the lessons above are connected to it—that Sarah Palin most needs to learn. She can make up her other deficiencies with study and practice. She will master the art of fielding the interviewer's question. She will become more polished as a speechmaker. She will be ready to name her favorite Founding Father next time around. But it will be in the crucible of character that her impact on American society will be defined.

She can certainly choose the low road. Most politicians do. There is money to be made and a crowd to be drawn by the politician on the attack, by the speaker who offers venom aflame for entertainment. It is a longstanding American art.

Yet if Palin decides to be a statesman—and surely this was the theme of the calling she sensed as a little girl—then she can rise to this nobility by the way she conducts herself. She can become a healer. She can build on love of country rather than hate for the opposing party, and she can grow as a person and take the nation with her as she does. If she will see her broadening global platform as an opportunity to do good in the world, she may leave a legacy loftier than mere short-term political victory. We are certainly in need of this as a nation, and she will certainly find herself in need of just such an elevated purpose as her years ahead unfold.

Epilogue

IN A LESS CRUEL WORLD, THE SARAH PALIN STORY MIGHT HAVE been regarded as the kind of tale that mothers tell their daughters to awaken slumbering greatness. She had grown up on what was left of an American frontier. Her father was a teacher, and her mother was a woman of grace and skill, both of whom were eager that she and her siblings not be among the mediocre and mindless multitudes. There were books and debates in the home, as there were disciplines and duties. At night, those who did not clear the table or do the dishes sang to the others as they worked. It sounds almost painfully quaint in the retelling, but it says much about the family culture from which she arose.

She became possessed of a fierce competitiveness, which evidenced itself most notably on the high school basketball court. She gained a lasting reputation for ending a championship game with a foul shot after suffering a fractured ankle. College loomed and she gave herself to it in fulfillment of her dreams and her parents' expectations. But she was uncertain, untethered. She attended five schools before finishing. Her drive surfaced, though, in her decision to compete in a humiliating beauty contest because it promised scholarship money she desperately needed. She did not win but did well enough to earn the money for school. It was the first of many victories. Soon, looks, a degree, and ambition landed her on television in her hometown.

She married, began having children, but recognized an inner fire that would not let her rest. She had been taught during all those years in church that she had a destiny to fulfill, some role of service to offer to mankind. It explained why she had been created as she was. She had long sensed this might be in politics, but nothing had presented itself. Then there was the school's PTA, and that opportunity on the city council, and finally she became mayor of her small town.

She served. She grew. She had still more babies. She supported her husband in his competitive dreams. She saw how her unusual state was run. She was appointed to a board to monitor petroleum policy but resigned when the corruption became too much. This is when she decided to run for governor. She did—on a financial shoe-string and on the strength of volunteer grandmothers and hockey moms—and she won.

By the time she started coming to national attention a few years later, she had already challenged the longstanding oil company control of her state, helped expose corruption in her own party, strengthened ethics requirements for state government, and earned the highest popularity rating of any Republican politician in the United States.

Hers was nearly the archetypical American story. She had risen through hard work, education, talent, and courage. She was married to her high school sweetheart, had five children, and had even chosen to give birth to a child with Down's syndrome when the prevailing culture would have urged differently. Pretty, feisty, and unshakably committed to her principles, she had the makings of a potent polit-ical force and a popular personality on the national scene.

Then too in a less cruel world, Sarah Palin's emergence on that national stage would have been celebrated. She held values respected by the vast majority of Americans—limited government, low taxes, strong defense, protection of the unborn, constitutional original intent, a tempered free market. And yet she was not unthinkingly right wing. Her politics were rooted in a suspicion of corporate power and in a belief in the good that government can do. She is not fully neocon or libertarian or religious Right or mainstream Republican. Her politics are too visceral and fundamental for any of these. She is a populist conservative, a woman who believes not in a conservatism of the parlor, the country club, or the debate society but in a real-world, street conservatism that is best for the people and in the grand tradition of the American way.

Had the chattering classes ears to hear, they would have noticed that while many Republicans were making excuses for Wall Street during the recent decline, Palin was on the attack. Few noticed too that she was almost vicious in her assault on BP as its oil leak poisoned our southeastern shores. And the Tea Party movement she helps to lead is as much about the rise of women and anger at corporate control of government and a coalition built across party lines as it is anything distinctly right wing. Palin's politics are not those of the conservatives from a generation before her, and in fact, she shares more than a few values with the American Left.

Liberalism ought to have noticed. Liberalism ought to have seen. But then liberalism in America today is not what it feigns to be. Liberalism, simply put, is not liberal. Nor is it about, as the Latin root of the word suggests, *being free*. Liberalism today is a statist orthodoxy that is deaf to moderation and that muzzles what it cannot control. It fears what Sarah Palin represents because she offers a critique of their edifice, a different and more moderate way.

Modern conservatives are equally deaf to what she might mean. Too wedded to corporate structures and to the pursuit of power at all costs, conservatives have laid aside much of the personal morality and American pillars that Palin seeks to restore. Thinking conservatives like Peggy Noonan—who might have been Palin's ally and should have been a mentor—can charge that Palin is shallow, but if they mean what they write in their columns, if they are committed to the values they claim to hold dear, then they should be grateful for Palin's presence in American politics. She will do them no harm and may serve to shape national policy debates in ways they can celebrate. The Tea Party movement shows what can happen when coalitions are built around specific shared values if all extraneous matters are kept at bay. The doctrinaire, cocktail-party conservatives of our day should take note.

So should the remnants of the religious Right. Having descended through personal immorality, lack of a generational vision, and a preference for king-making over the politics of servanthood, it is time for this movement to return to the better angels of its nature. Its strengths have historically been in its call for moral government, in its defense of First Amendment original intent, and in its pastoring of leaders on both sides of the aisles. These strengths and their possibilities are not lost, and Sarah Palin may well be an ally. But she is no messiah, no savior of a crumbling religious edifice. She is simply a fellow believer serving her God in the public sphere. Indeed, she could use the input of this movement when it is at its best and not seeking power for its own sake.

She will need this input because there will come another campaign, another crusade of some kind before a watching world. Before that day, she will learn. She will grow. She will watch the films of her failures and storm the room and determine that it will never happen again. She will study and rehearse and improve, perhaps becoming what she might have been had she not been sent onto the field too soon. She believes she has a destiny. There is work for her to do, she understands: work ordained by God. And she loves her country. She believes it is in crisis, but she does not see Churchills on the horizon. She is willing and does not fear the battle. When you care about your cause, you sound a certain trumpet of your own when all other trumpets dim.

Acknowledgments

AMONG THE DELIGHTS OF THE WRITING LIFE ARE THE PEOPLE whose wisdom, struggles, and memories become indelibly imprinted upon each page of each book that an author has the privilege of writing. This book has been no different, and the authors are grateful beyond words to those who have left their mark upon its pages.

During a frigid but fascinating trek through Alaska, we had the privilege of sipping coffee in the home of Chuck and Sally Heath, Sarah Palin's parents. They were gracious and helpful, and we were touched by their hospitality as much as we were by their lives. Paul and Edna Riley opened their home as well as their story to us and spent tender hours recounting their own Alaskan sojourn. How thankful we are. Pastor Larry Kroon told us the story of faith in his city and also introduced us to John McPhee's *Coming Into the Country*, which changed us. Dan and Carol Ryan told us their tearful tale of life in Wasilla and of their joyous life as friends of the Heaths. Bill McAllister, the gifted journalist who eventually went to work for Governor Palin, helped us understand Alaskan politics and the McCain/Palin campaign from a unique perspective. We are grateful to each of these, for their kindness, their passion, and their graciousness.

Ted Boatsman and Theron Horne helped us understand both life in Wasilla and the spiritual life of Sarah Palin with a depth that few could have offered. Their gifts and fortitude have shaped much of the story in this book. We are also grateful for the time afforded us by Bishop Thomas Muthee of Kenya. Bob Heckman and Guy Rodgers, both with vast experience on the faith side of John McCain's political life, were wise, insightful, and generous. And Kevin Ikenberry, Tulsa lawyer and Roman Catholic theologian, consulted with us on the pre–Vatican II Rite of Baptism. Thank you each.

We spent fascinating hours in both the Dorothy Page Museum in Wasilla and the Anchorage Museum at Rasmuson Center. We are grateful to the staffs of these facilities as well as to the thousands like them throughout the nation.

It is a delight to work with the fine staff and publishers of Strang Communications. Barbara Dycus, friend and editor, has made this project much more than it would have been without her, and Tessie DeVore, executive vice president of the book group at Strang, is ever the skilled negotiator and whip-cracker. Woodley Auguste has served us not only with his gift for encouragement and public relations but has also regaled us with his experience as a black man in Alaska where, as he insists, he doubled the state's African American presence.

Finally, David Holland would like to thank his wife, Tracy, for extraordinary patience and support and frequent access to her copy-editing superpowers. He would also like to thank Betty Holland, a pioneer woman in her own right, for her consistent support and encouragement throughout this project and for being the finest example of a woman of faith and values he has known.

Stephen Mansfield is grateful for the fine team at Chartwell Literary Group (ChartwellLiterary.com) and at The Mansfield Group (MansfieldGroup.com), who have made this project a joy. Most of all Stephen is simply grateful that Beverly Mansfield exists.

Notes

INTRODUCTION

1. Stanley Kurtz, "Angry Talk," *National Review Online*, January 2, 2007, http://article.nationalreview.com/302063/angry-talk/stanley-kurtz (accessed May 25, 2010).

2. Discussion with author, March 15, 2010.

3. Noel Sheppard, "Matthews Attacks Palin for 12 Minutes: 'Can a Palm Reader be President?' 'Is She a Balloon Head?'" Newsbusters.org, http://newsbusters.org/blogs/noel-sheppard/2010/02/08/matthews-attacks-sarah-palm-reader-palin-she-balloon-head (accessed June 3, 2010).

4. Andrew Sullivan, "The Filter That Protects Palin From Scrutiny," TheAtlantic.com, April 10, 2010, http://andrewsullivan.theatlantic.com/the_daily_dish/2010/04/the-filter-that-protects-palin-from-scrutiny.html (accessed May 27, 2010).

5. Peter Wood, *A Bee in the Mouth: Anger in America Now* (New York: Encounter Books, 2007).

6. Demographia.com, "Metropolitan Regions Over 1,000,000 in 2000: Change From 1950," http://www.demographia.com/db-usmet19502000.pdf (accessed June 3, 2010); Wendell Cox, "Suburbs and Cities: The Unexpected Truth," Newgeography.com, May 16, 2009, http://www.newgeography.com/content/00805-suburbs-and-cities-the-unexpected-truth (accessed June 3, 2010).

7. Maureen Dowd, "Now, Sarah's Folly," *New York Times*, July 4, 2009, http://www.nytimes.com/2009/07/05/opinion/05dowd.html?_r=1&partner=rssnyt&emc=rss (accessed May 25, 2010).

8. Mitch Marconi, "Sarah Palin 'Trailer Trash' Photos: Hoop Earrings by John McCain's Side," *The Post Chronicle*, September 1, 2008, http://www.postchronicle.com/cgi-bin/artman/exec/view.cgi?archive=91&num=168763 (accessed May 25, 2010).

9. Jon Meacham, "The Palin Problem," *Newsweek*, October 4, 2008.

10. David Carr, "How Sarah Palin Became a Brand," *New York Times*, April 4, 2010.

11. Thomas Jefferson, Query XIX, *Notes on the State of Virginia*, chapter 19, http://xroads.virginia.edu/~hyper/jefferson/ch19.html (accessed May 25, 2010).

12. Juan Cole, "What's the Difference Between Palin and Muslim Fundamentalists? Lipstick," *Salon*, September 9, 2008, http://www .salon.com/news/opinion/feature/2008/09/09/palin_fundamentalist (accessed June 3, 2010).

13. Max Blumenthal, "Inside Sarah's Church," *The Daily Beast*, September 5, 2009, http://www.thedailybeast.com/blogs-and-stories/ 2009-09-05/inside-sarahs-church/ (accessed June 3, 2010).

14. James Howard Kunstler, "We're Weimar," Kunstler.com, February 8, 2010, http://kunstler.com/blog/2010/02/were-weimar.html (accessed June 3, 2010).

15. Ibid.

16. Ryan Powers, "Pelosi: Tea Parties Are Part of an 'Astroturf' Campaign by 'Some of the Wealthiest People in America,'" ThinkProgress.org, April 15, 2009, http://thinkprogress.org/ 2009/04/15/pelosi-astroturf/ (accessed May 25, 2010).

17. Quinnipiac University, "Tea Party Could Hurt GOP in Congressional Races, Quinnipiac University National Poll Finds; Dems Trail 2-Way Races, but Win if Tea Party Runs," March 24, 2010, http://www.quinnipiac.edu/x1295.xml?ReleaseID=1436 (accessed May 25, 2010).

18. Institute of Social and Economic Research, "Alaska's People and Economy: 1867–2009," *UA Research Summary No. 15*, September 2009, http://www.iser.uaa.alaska.edu/Publications/formal/rsummary/ UA_RS15final_eversion.pdf (accessed May 6, 2010).

CHAPTER 1
ROOTS OF FAITH AND DARING

1. Robert A. Heinlein, *Time Enough for Love* (New York: Ace Books, 1973), 251.

2. United States Geological Society, "Historic Earthquakes: Largest Earthquake in Alaska," http://earthquake.usgs.gov/earthquakes/states/ events/1964_03_28.php (accessed May 25, 2010).

3. Kevin Ikenberry, Tulsa lawyer and Roman Catholic theologian, consulted with us on the pre-Vatican II Rite of Baptism.

CHAPTER 2
PROFILE: THE GREAT LAND

1. John McPhee, *Coming Into the Country* (New York: Farrar, Straus and Giroux, 1991), 244–245.

2. David McCullough, *Brave Companions* (New York: Simon & Schuster, 1992), x.

3. "Sarah Palin's Farewell Address—Full Transcript," *Huffington Post*, July 27, 2009, http://www.huffingtonpost.com/akmuckraker/ sarah-palins-farewell-add_b_245215.html (accessed May 4, 2010).

CHAPTER 3
WARRIOR RISING

1. Henry David Thoreau, "Conclusion," in *Walden* (Boston, MA: Beacon Press, 1854, 2004), 303.

2. Sarah Palin, *Going Rogue: An American Life* (New York: HarperCollins, 2009), 8.

3. Ibid., 9.

4. Kaylene Johnson, *Sarah* (Chicago: Tyndale House, 2008), 22.

5. Emil Zapotek, as quoted at AbsoluteAstronomy.com, "Emil Zapotek," http://www.absoluteastronomy.com/topics/Emil_Z%C3% Altopek (accessed May 25, 2010).

6. Ibid.

7. Palin, *Going Rogue*, 41.

CHAPTER 4
THE TURNING

1. John Heilemann and Mark Halperin, *Game Change* (New York: HarperCollins, 2010), 364.

2. Palin, *Going Rogue*, 47.

3. Revelation 3:15–16, NAS, Catholic Edition, 1970.

4. John 3:5–7, NAS.

5. General Council of the Assemblies of God, "Baptism in the Holy Spirit," http://www.ag.org/top/Beliefs/gendoct_02_baptismhs.cfm (accessed June 4, 2010).

6. Author interview with Theron Horne, March 5, 2010.

Chapter 5
Profile: To Be Pentecostal

1. Grant McClung, "Pentecostals: The Sequel," *Christianity Today*, April 1, 2006, http://www.christianitytoday.com/ct/2006/april/7.30 .html (accessed May 5, 2010).

2. Ibid.

3. John Thomas Nichol, *The Pentecostals* (Plainfield, NJ: Logos, 1966), 33.

4. McClung, "Pentecostals: The Sequel."

5. Nichol, *The Pentecostals*, 34.

6. David M. Barrett, World Evangelization Research Center, http://www.gem-werc.org/. Barrett projects that by 2020 the figure will reach 811 million. Barrett is the author of *The Encyclopedia of Christianity* (New York: Oxford University Press, 2002).

Chapter 6
Todd

1. Richard F. Burton, *The Kasîdah Of Hâjî Abdû El-Yezdî* (1870).

2. Levi Johnston, "Me and Mrs. Palin," *Vanity Fair*, October 2009, http://www.vanityfair.com/politics/features/2009/10/levi -johnston200910?currentPage=3 (accessed May 11, 2010).

3. Palin, *Going Rogue*, 179.

Section 1 Afterword
Four Truths From Sarah Palin's Beginnings

1. NewsCore, "Palin Supports Arizona's Immigration Law," myFOXphoenix.com, May 16, 2010, http://www.myfoxphoenix.com/ dpps/news/palin-supports-arizona-immigration-law-dpgonc-km -20100516_7565711 (accessed May 25, 2010).

2. Dianna Parker, "Gibbs Knocks Down Palin's Charge That Obama's Response to Oil Spill Is Connected to Donations," MediaMatters.org, May 23, 2010, http://mediamatters.org/blog/201005230009 (accessed May 25, 2010).

3. Dana Milbank, "A Thank-You for 18 Million Cracks in the Glass Ceiling," *Washington Post*, June 8, 2008, accessed at http://www.washingtonpost.com/wp-dyn/content/article/2008/06/07/AR2008060701879.html, May 25, 2010.

4. H. Seidelman and J. Turner, *The Inuit Imagination: Arctic Myth and Sculpture* (British Columbia: Douglas & McIntyre, 1993).

5. Palin, *Going Rogue*, 47.

CHAPTER 7
INTO THE FRAY

1. Mao Tse-Tung, "On Protracted War," *Selected Works of Mao Tse-Tung*, vol. II (Peking, China: Foreign Language Press, 1938), 152–153.

2. Verifiable.com, "USA Divorce Rates by State," http://verifiable.com/app#/data_sets/2356 (accessed May 6, 2010).

3. Julie Bosman, "Palin Aides Release Her Medical History," *New York Times*, November 4, 2008, http://www.nytimes.com/2008/11/04/us/politics/04medical.html (accessed May 6, 2010).

4. Noam Scheiber, "Barracuda: The Resentments of Sarah Palin," *New Republic*, October 22, 2008, http://www.tnr.com/article/barracuda (accessed May 6, 2010).

CHAPTER 8
REALIGNMENT: THE CULTURE WAR COMES TO THE VALLEY

1. Francis Schaffer, *How Should We Then Live?* (Grand Rapids, MI: Fleming H. Revell Co., 1976), 19.

2. Max Blumenthal, *Republican Gomorrah: Inside the Movement That Shattered the Party* (New York: Nation Books, 2009), 10–11.

3. Palin, *Going Rogue*, 88.

CHAPTER 9
THE PALIN POLITICAL BRAND

1. William F. Buckley, "Our Mission Statement," *National Review*, November 19, 1955, http://article.nationalreview.com/346187/our -mission-statement/william-f-buckley-jr (accessed June 8, 2010).

2. David Brooks, "Why Experience Matters," *New York Times*, September 15, 2008, http://www.nytimes.com/2008/09/16/opinion/ 16brooks.html (accessed June 8, 2010).

3. As reported in Danny Shea, "David Brooks: Sarah Palin 'Represents a Fatal Cancer to the Republican Party,'" HuffingtonPost .com, October 8, 2008, http://www.huffingtonpost.com/2008/10/08/ david-brooks-sarah-palin_n_133001.html (accessed June 8, 2010).

4. Ibid.

5. William F. Buckley, *Rumbles Left and Right* (New York: Putnam's Sons, 1993), 134.

6. Peggy Noonan, "A Farewell to Harms," *Wall Street Journal*, July 10, 2009, http://online.wsj.com/article/SB124716984620819351.html (accessed June 8, 2010).

7. Danielle Crittenden, @DCrittenden1, Twitter.com, April 15, 2010, 8:43 p.m., http://twitter.com/DCrittenden1 (accessed June 8, 2010).

8. Buckley, "Our Mission Statement."

9. Allan Bloom, *The Closing of the American Mind* (New York: Simon & Schuster, 1988), 217.

10. Quinnipiac University, "Tea Party Could Hurt GOP in Congressional Races, Quinnipiac University National Poll Finds; Dems Trail 2-Way Races, but Win if Tea Party Runs."

11. Paul Harvey, *Remember These Things* (Chicago: The Heritage Foundation, 1952), 9.

12. Richard Corliss, "Paul Harvey: The End of the Story," *Time*, March 1, 2009, http://www.time.com/time/arts/article/0,8599,1882444 ,00.html (accessed May 5, 2010).

13. NationalReview.com, "The 100 Best Non-Fiction Books of the Century," http://old.nationalreview.com/100best/100_books.html (accessed May 25, 2010).

14. C. S. Lewis, *The Abolition of Man* (New York: HarperCollins, 2001), 26.

CHAPTER 10
"IF I DIE, I DIE"

1. Milton Friedman, *Capitalism and Freedom* (Chicago: University of Chicago Press, 1962, 2002), 2.

2. Institute of Social and Economic Research, "Alaska's People and Economy: 1867–2009."

3. Robert Douglas Mead, *Journeys Down the Line: Building the Trans-Alaska Pipeline* (New York: Doubleday, 1978), 349.

4. Alaska Permanent Fund Corporation, "Accountability to Alaskans, for Alaskans," http://www.apfc.org/home/Media/aboutAPFC/POMVinsrt.pdf (accessed May 6, 2010).

5. Alaska Permanent Fund Corporation, "What Is the Alaska Permanent Fund Corporation?" http://www.apfc.org/home/Content/aboutFund/aboutPermFund.cfm (accessed May 6, 2010); Alaska Permanent Fund Corporation, "Dividend Amounts," http://www.apfc.org/home/Content/dividend/dividendamounts.cfm (accessed June 8, 2010).

6. Yereth Rosen, "Alaska Sees $1.25 Billion Budget Gap on Oil Price Drop," Reuters.com, February 19, 2009, http://www.reuters.com/article/idUSTRE51J02J20090220 (accessed May 6, 2010).

7. Kay Cashman and Kristi Nelson, *Sarah Takes on Big Oil* (Anchorage, AK: PNA Publishing, 2008), 45.

8. Palin, *Going Rogue*, 98.

9. Esther 4:14.

CHAPTER 11
FIVE SMOOTH STONES

1. Dr. Robert Jarvik, inventor of the Jarvik-7 artificial heart.

2. Lori Backes, "Follow the Money to Governor's Gas Deal," *Anchorage Daily News*, March 3, 2006.

3. Lynne Truss, *Eats, Shoots and Leaves: The Zero Tolerance Approach to Punctuation* (New York: Gotham, 2003), 3.

4. CNN.com, "Sarah Palin Speaks at Tea Party Convention," CNN Newsroom Transcripts, aired February 6, 2010, http://transcripts.cnn.com/TRANSCRIPTS/1002/06/cnr.09.html (accessed May 26, 2010).

5. 1 Samuel 17:40.

6. Palin, *Going Rogue*, 106–107.

7. An opinion piece by Sarah Palin, which appeared in the *Mat-Su Frontiersman* in 2006, cited in Cashman and Nelson, *Sarah Takes on Big Oil*, 15.

8. Cashman and Nelson, *Sarah Takes on Big Oil*, 27.

9. Ibid., 53.

10. Ibid., 23.

11. Sarah Palin, "Oil, Gas Deal Should Show 'Maximum Benefit for All Alaskans,'" *Mat-Su Valley Frontiersman*, March 19, 2006, http://www.frontiersman.com/articles/2006/03/19/news/opinion/opinion2.txt (accessed May 26, 2010).

12. Author interview with Bill McAllister, March 5, 2010.

13. Cited in Cashman and Nelson, *Sarah Takes on Big Oil*, 47.

14. Pat Forgey, "Governor Travel Shot Up With Murkowski's Jet, Plummets With Palin," *Juneau Empire*, April 8, 2008, http://www.juneauempire.com/stories/040808/sta_267202920.shtml (accessed May 11, 2010).

15. Fred Barnes, "The Most Popular Governor," *Weekly Standard*, July 16, 2007, http://weeklystandard.com/Content/Public/Articles/000/000/013/851orcjq.asp (accessed May 26, 2010).

CHAPTER 12
MCCAIN

1. Author interview with Bob Heckman, March 17, 2010.

2. John McCain, *Faith of My Fathers* (New York: Random House, 1999), 206.

3. Ibid., 332.

4. Author interview with Bob Heckman, March 17, 2010.

5. Ibid.

CHAPTER 13
PROFILE: FAITH AND THE ELECTION OF 2008

1. *Ebony*, "William Clay: a Militant With a Knack for Wins," February 1969, 65, http://books.google.com/books?id=9eEDAAAAM BAJ&pg=PA65&lpg=PA65&dq (accessed May 7, 2010).

2. WashingtonPost.com, "Transcript: Illinois Senate Candidate Barack Obama," July 27, 2004, http://www.washingtonpost.com/wp -dyn/articles/A19751-2004Jul27.html (accessed June 9, 2010).

3. *Zorach v. Clauson*, 343 U.S. 306 (1952); transcript of decision available at http://scholar.google.com/scholar_case?case=486580129202 9366499&hl=en&as_sdt=2&as_vis=1&oi=scholar (accessed June 9, 2010).

4. *Everson v. Board of Education*, 330 U.S. 1 (1947).

5. George W. Bush, *A Charge to Keep* (New York: Harper Paperbacks, 2001), 122–123.

6. The American Presidency Project, "George W. Bush: Remarks at the National Day of Prayer and Remembrance Service, September 14, 2001," http://www.presidency.ucsb.edu/ws/index.php?pid=63645&st =&st1= (accessed June 9, 2010).

7. FOXNews.com, "Bush Says Creation 'Not Incompatible'" With Evolution," interview with Christine McFadden on ABC's *Nightline*, September 8, 2008, http://www.foxnews.com/politics/2008/12/09/ bush-says-creation-incompatible-evolution (accessed May 7, 2010).

8. Barack Obama, "Call to Renewal Keynote Address," June 28, 2006, BarackObama.com, http://www.barackobama.com/2006/06/28/ call_to_renewal_keynote_address.php (accessed May 7, 2010).

9. Ibid.

10. Ibid.

11. Barna Group, "Born Again Voters No Longer Favor Republican Candidates," February 4, 2008, http://www.barna.org/barna-update/ article/13-culture/49-born-again-voters-no-longer-favor-republican -candidates?q=evangelical (accessed June 9, 2010).

12. Pew Forum on Religion and Public Life, "How the News Media Covered Religion in the General Election," November 20, 2008, http://www.pewforum.org/Politics-and-Elections/How-the

-News-Media-Covered-Religion-in-the-General-Election.aspx (accessed May 7, 2010).

CHAPTER 14
GOING ROGUE?

1. Matthew 5:11, 14.

2. Manya A. Brachear, "How Religion Guides Palin," *Chicago Tribune*, September 6, 2008, http://www.chicagotribune.com/news/ nationworld/chi-palin-religion_06sep06,0,3371419.story (accessed May 7, 2010).

3. CNN.com, "Sen. John McCain Attacks Pat Robertson, Jerry Falwell, Republican Establishment as Harming GOP Ideals," February 28, 2000, http://transcripts.cnn.com/TRANSCRIPTS/0002/28/se.01 .html (accessed May 7, 2010).

4. Sam Howe Verhovek, "Is There Room on the Republican Ticket for Another Bush?" *New York Times Magazine*, September 13, 1998.

5. Bush, *A Charge to Keep*, 122–123.

6. Barack Obama, *Dreams From My Father* (New York: Crown Publishers, 2004), 155.

7. Barack Obama, *Audacity of Hope* (New York: Crown Publishers, 2006), 206.

8. Obama, *Dreams From My Father*, 287.

9. Ibid., 208.

10. Cathleen Falsani, "I Have a Deep Faith," *Chicago Sun Times*, April 5, 2004, http://www.suntimes.com/news/falsani/ 726619,obamafalsani040504.article (accessed June 9, 2010); Sarah Pulliam and Ted Olson, "Q&A: Barack Obama," *Christianity Today*, January 2008, http://www.christianitytoday.com/ct/2008/januaryweb -only/104-32.0.html (accessed June 9, 2010).

11. Palin, *Going Rogue*, 22.

12. S. E. Cupp, *Losing Our Religion* (New York: Threshold Editions, 2010).

13. Quoted in R. E. McMaster, *Wealth for All* (Whitefish: A.N., Inc., 1982), 85.

14. Martin Luther King Jr., "A Knock at Midnight," in *A Knock at Midnight: Inspiration from the Great Sermons of Reverend Martin Luther King Jr.* (New York: Grand Central Publishing, 2000), 72–73.

CHAPTER 15
THE POLITICS OF PERSONAL DESTRUCTION

1. As cited in Susan Crabtree, "Where Do I Go to Get My Reputation Back?" *Insight on the News*, February 19,1996, http://findarticles.com/p/articles/mi_m1571/is_n7_v12/ai_18008947/ (accessed May 27, 2010).

2. Chris Geidner, "Edward Kennedy's America and the Bork Nomination," LawDork.net, August 30, 2009, http://lawdork.net/2009/08/30/edward-kennedys-america-and-the-bork-nomination/ (accessed May 27, 2010).

3. Joan Walsh, "James Carville," *Salon*, March 11, 2002, http://www.salon.com/people/feature/2002/03/11/carville (accessed June 18, 2010).

4. Tom Delay with Stephen Mansfield, *No Retreat, No Surrender* (New York: Sentinel HC, 2007).

5. AssociatedContent.com, "Sarah Palin Defending Many Lawsuits," April 14, 2009, http://www.associatedcontent.com/article/1642957/sarah_palin_defending_many_lawsuits.html?cat=17 (accessed May 27, 2010).

6. Philip Rucker and Eli Saslow, "Gov. Palin Says She Will Quit, Citing Probes, Family Needs," *Washington Post*, July 4, 2009, http://www.washingtonpost.com/wp-dyn/content/article/2009/07/03/AR2009070301738.html (accessed May 27, 2010).

7. Mark Twain, *The Wit and Wisdom of Mark Twain: A Book of Quotations* (New York: Harper Perennial, 2005), 35.

8. Joan K. Morris, "Trends in Down's Syndrome Live Births and Antenatal Diagnoses in England and Wales From 1989 to 2008: Analysis of Data From the National Down Syndrome Cytogenetic Register," *British Medical Journal* 339 (October 26, 2009): http://www.bmj.com/cgi/content/full/339/oct26_3/b3794 2009 (accessed May 11, 2010).

9. Andrew Sullivan, "The Filter That Protects Palin From Scrutiny," *The Atlantic*, April 24, 2010, http://andrewsullivan.theatlantic.com/ the_daily_dish/2010/04/the-filter-that-protects-palin-from-scrutiny .html (accessed June 10, 2010).

10. Michelle Malkin, "Kooky Politics," December 5, 2008, National Review Online, http://article.nationalreview.com/380142/kooky -politics/michelle-malkin (accessed May 7, 2010).

11. Queerty.com, "Andrew Sullivan's Sarah Palin Obsession is Exhausting," http://www.queerty.com/andrew-sullivans-sarah-palin -obsession-is-exhausting-20091208/ (accessed May 7, 2010).

12. Johnston, "Me and Mrs. Palin."

13. RockyMountainNews.com, "Rocky Truth Patrol: Palin on Evolution vs. Creationism," September 2, 2008, http://blogs .rockymountainnews.com/dnc_truth_patrol/archives/2008/09/palin -on-evolution-vs-creation.html (accessed June 10, 2010).

14. Compiled from Morton Montgomery, "Reasons Why Sarah Palin Is a Terrible Threat to America," DailyKos.com, October 29, 2008, http://www.dailykos.com/storyonly/2008/10/29/95322/578 (accessed June 18, 2010); Loonwatch.com, "Sarah Palin Supports Stoning and Slavery?" May 14, 2010, http://www.loonwatch.com/ 2010/05/sarah-palin-supports-stoning-and-slavery/?utm_source=feed burner&utm_medium=feed&utm_campaign=Feed%3A+loonwatch+%2 8loonwatch.com%29 (accessed June 18, 2010).

CHAPTER 16
PALIN AND THE FRONTRUNNERS FOR 2012

1. FreeRepublic.com, "Tea Party Total Head Count," http://www .freerepublic.com/focus/news/2229982/posts?page=482 (accessed May 27, 2010).

2. Jane Devin, "The Christian Right Killed the Republican Party," *Huffington Post*, October 27, 2008, http://www.huffingtonpost.com/ jane-devin/the-christian-right-kille_b_137946.html (accessed June 10, 2010).

3. Jon Meacham, "The End of Christian America," *Newsweek*, April 4, 2009, http://www.newsweek.com/id/192583 (accessed June 10, 2010).

4. Max Blumenthal, *Republican Gomorrah* (New York: Nation Books, 2009).

5. David Kirby and David Boaz, "Policy Analysis: The Libertarian Vote," October 18, 2006, CATO Institute, http://www.cato.org/pub _display.php?pub_id=6715 (accessed May 7, 2010).

6. Katherine Q. Seelye, "Ron Paul Wins CPAC Straw Poll," NewYorkTimes.com, February 20, 2010, http://thecaucus.blogs .nytimes.com/2010/02/20/ron-paul-wins-cpac-straw-poll/ (accessed May 10, 2010).

7. Jon Cohen and Phillip Rucker, "Poll Finds Most Americans Are Unhappy With Government," *Washington Post*, http://www .washingtonpost.com/wp-dyn/content/article/2010/02/10/ AR2010021004708.html (accessed June 10, 2010).

8. Rasmussen Reports, "Election 2008: 43% Would Never Vote for Mormon Candidate," November 20, 2006, http://www .rasmussenreports.com/public_content/politics/top_stories/election _2008_43_would_never_vote_for_mormon_candidate (accessed May 10, 2010).

9. Kheilil Bouarrou, "Mitt Romney and Sarah Palin Presidential Ticket?" Examiner.com, April 16, 2010, http://www .examiner.com/x-39852-DC-RNC-Examiner~y2010m4d16-Mitt-Romney--Sarah-Palin-Presidential-Ticket?cid=exrss-DC-RNC-Examiner (accessed May 10, 2010).

10. Ron Paul, "Statement of Faith," *Covenant News*, July 21, 2007, http://www.covenantnews.com/ronpaul070721.htm (accessed June 10, 2010).

11. John Amato, "Newt Gingrich 2012?" CrooksandLiars.com, http://crooksandliars.com/karoli/newt-gingrich-2012 (accessed June 10, 2010).

12. Sarah Pulliam, "Q&A: Newt Gingrich," *Christianity Today*, April 17, 2009.

13. Ibid.

SECTION 3 AFTERWORD
SEVEN THINGS SARAH PALIN NEEDS TO KNOW

1. Winston Churchill to his wife, Clementine, in 1916, cited in Kati Marton, *Hidden Power: Presidential Marriages That Shaped Our History* (New York: Random Books, 2001), 4.

2. FOXNews.com, "Sarah Palin on 'Glenn Beck,'" January 14, 2010, http://www.foxnews.com/story/0,2933,583028,00.html (accessed May 10, 2010).

3. E. Stanley Jones, cited in Stephen Mansfield, *Never Give In* (Nashville, TN: Cumberland House Publishing, Inc., 1995), 115.

4. Psalm 16:6.

INDEX

Bloom, Allan 104, 106, 108
Blumenthal, Max 95–96, 195, 197
Boatsman, Ted 45–46, 48
Bob Jones University 165
Bork, Robert 104, 180
born again, born-again 44–45, 47, 156, 160, 167, 171, 209
Boston Marathon 33
breast lesion 81
Bristol Bay 66, 87, 101, 124
British Medical Journal 185
British Petroleum, BP 68–69, 73, 118, 135, 217
Brooks, David 105–106, 195
Brooks Brothers Alaskan(s) 83, 85
Brown, Scott 197
Buckley, William F. 104, 106–107
Burton, Richard Francis 63
Bush, George H. W. 86, 163, 172, 206
Bush, George W. 71, 92, 105, 154, 163–166, 171–173, 175–176, 196, 207–209, 212

C

Cady, Max 55
California 22, 120, 195
Cape Fear 55
Capitalism and Freedom 115
Carney, Michelle 35–36, 83
Carney, Nick 83–88, 100, 113, 126
Carter, Jimmy 93–94, 121, 160, 209
Carville, James 181
Catholic church in Wasilla 43–44

Chambers, Whittaker 104
Chávez, Hugo 164
Cheechakos 28–29, 85
Chinook 28
Christian Coalition 97
Christian media 95, 176
Christian Scientist 14
Christ the King Roman Catholic Church, Richland, Washington 11
Chronicles of Narnia series, The 110
Chugach mountains 24
Churchill, Winston 22, 71, 179, 207, 218
Church in the Wildwood 43
City and Man, The 104
Clay, William 159
Clinton, Bill 86, 94, 98, 206
Clinton, Hillary 73, 98, 206
Closing of the American Mind, The 104
Columbia Basin College 13, 15
Columbia University 173
Common Cause organization 181
common sense conservatism 101, 106–108
Complete Book of Running, The 33
Concerned Women for America 95, 97
Conflict of Visions, A 104
ConocoPhillips 135
conservative(s) 4, 6–7, 87, 92–94, 97–98, 103–108, 110–111, 135, 145, 149–155, 160, 163–164, 167, 181, 186, 193, 195–198, 200, 204–205, 210–212, 216–218

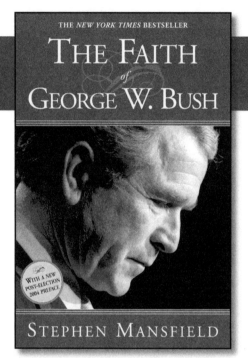
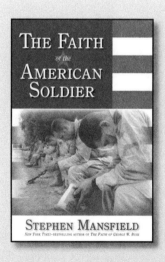

FREE NEWSLETTERS
TO HELP EMPOWER YOUR LIFE

Why subscribe today?

☐ **DELIVERED DIRECTLY TO YOU.** All you have to do is open your inbox and read.

☐ **EXCLUSIVE CONTENT.** We cover the news overlooked by the mainstream press.

☐ **STAY CURRENT.** Find the latest court rulings, revivals, and cultural trends.

☐ **UPDATE OTHERS.** Easy to forward to friends and family with the click of your mouse.

CHOOSE THE E-NEWSLETTER THAT INTERESTS YOU MOST:

- Christian news
- Daily devotionals
- Spiritual empowerment
- And much, much more

SIGN UP AT: **http://freenewsletters.charismamag.com**

8178